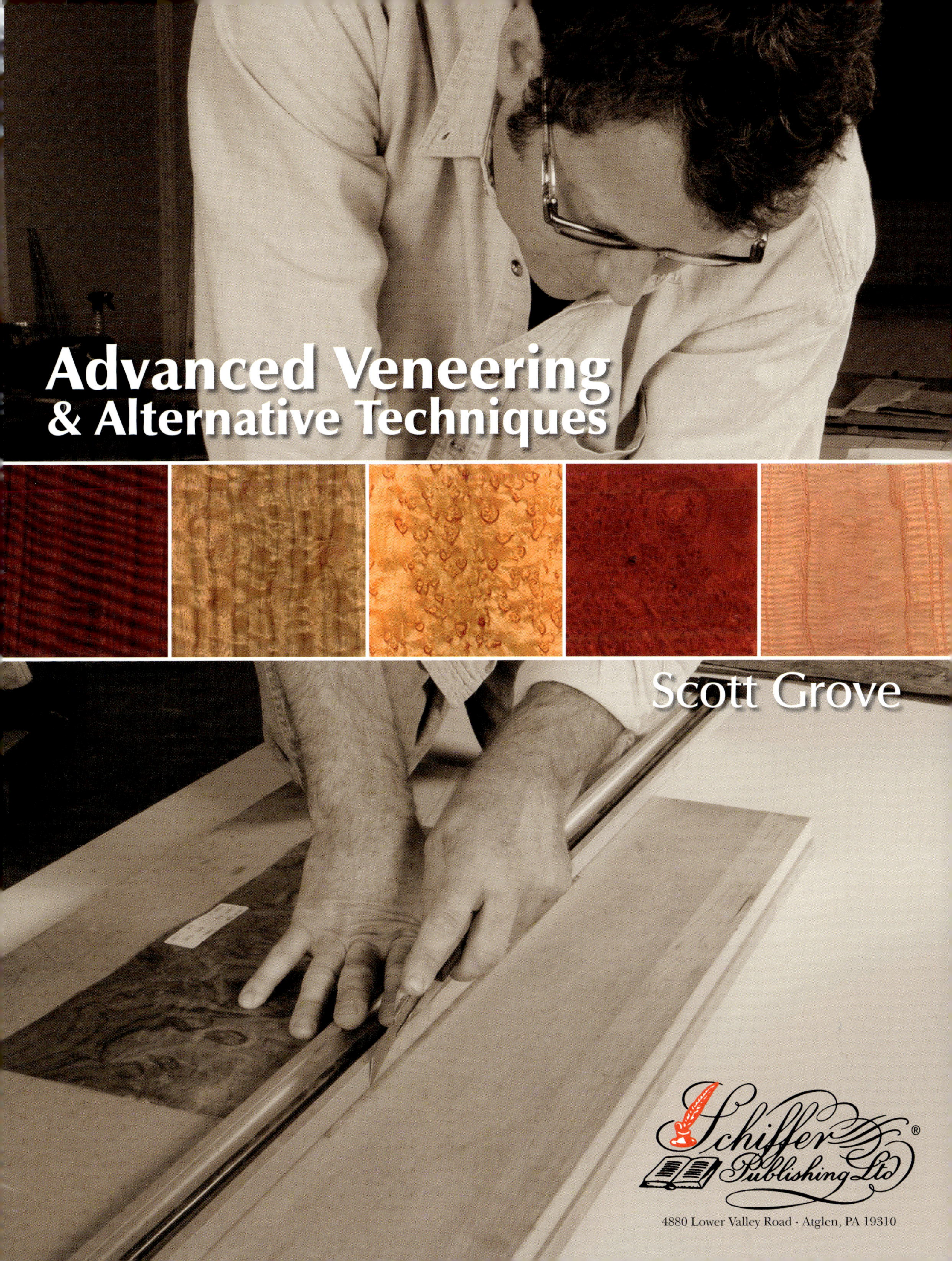
Advanced Veneering
& Alternative Techniques
Scott Grove
Schiffer Publishing Ltd
4880 Lower Valley Road · Atglen, PA 19310

DISCLAIMER:

Most of the items and products in this book may be covered by various copyrights, trademarks, and logotypes. Their use herein is for identification purposes only. All rights are reserved by their respective owners.

The text and products pictured in this book are from the collection of the author of this book, its publisher, or various private collectors. This book is not sponsored, endorsed, or otherwise affiliated with any of the companies whose products are represented herein.

They include:

Behlen's
Betterbond
Blendal
Dremel
Exacto
Famowood
Hybond
J.E. Moser's
Mas Exposies
Masonite
Mylar
Scotchbrite
Stir
System Three
Titebond

Library of Congress Control Number: 2011932785

Designed by John P. Cheek
Type set in ZapfHumnst Ult BT/ ZapfHumnst BT

ISBN: 978-0-7643-3846-5
Printed in the United States of America

Schiffer Books are available at special discounts for bulk purchases for sales promotions or premiums. Special editions, including personalized covers, corporate imprints, and excerpts can be created in large quantities for special needs. For more information contact the publisher:

Published by Schiffer Publishing Ltd.
4880 Lower Valley Road
Atglen, PA 19310
Phone: (610) 593-1777; Fax: (610) 593-2002
E-mail: Info@schifferbooks.com

For the largest selection of fine reference books on this and related subjects, please visit our website at
www.schifferbooks.com
We are always looking for people to write books on new and related subjects. If you have an idea for a book please contact us at: proposals@schifferbooks.com

This book may be purchased from the publisher.
Include $5.00 for shipping.
Please try your bookstore first.
You may write for a free catalog.

In Europe, Schiffer books are distributed by
Bushwood Books
6 Marksbury Ave.
Kew Gardens
Surrey TW9 4JF England
Phone: 44 (0) 20 8392 8585; Fax: 44 (0) 20 8392 9876
E-mail: info@bushwoodbooks.co.uk
Website: www.bushwoodbooks.co.uk

I dedicate this book to my Lionheart,
Nancy Napurski

Acknowledgments

I give my sincerest thanks to a number of people for their support, time and patience:

First, to Marc Adams of the Marc Adams School of Woodworking for introducing me to Peter Schiffer of Schiffer Publishing. To my students who allow me to help them "find the line," cross it, and discover ways to move it; they provide me with an opportunity to advance my own personal growth and woodworking as a whole.

My humblest thanks to a number of industry veterans for their patience, time and contributions. To Certainly Wood Inc. and Greg Ingel for technical support and superb quality material used in this book. To Daryl Keil of Vacuum Systems for his insight, very interesting trivia, information, and extensive knowledge. To John Van Brusell of Veneer Systems for verification and equipment knowledge support. And to Mike Maier, vice president of operations of the Danzer Specialty Veneers' veneer mill, for a personal plant tour and follow up questions.

Thanks to a number of associates who contributed and/or allowed me to photograph equipment and pick their brains: Andrew Muggleton, Chuck Wright of North Creek Woodworking, Seth Eshelman, John Dodd and Wendell Castle.

Thank you to one of my oldest and dearest friends, Khym Kaupelis, for patient proofreading and honest and kind critique. To my son Zachary Grove, a gifted writer, for numerous readings and edits. To my son Sean Grove, for his support and help in the shop. Both gave up valuable time spent with their dad while I was consumed with my life's work as well as this project.

Lastly and most importantly, to my soul mate, Nancy Napurski. If not for her patience and diligent editing, this book would have never come to fruition. For the tedious re-reads, checks, tweaks, and sacrificing days and nights to complete on time, I love you and thank you.

CONTENTS

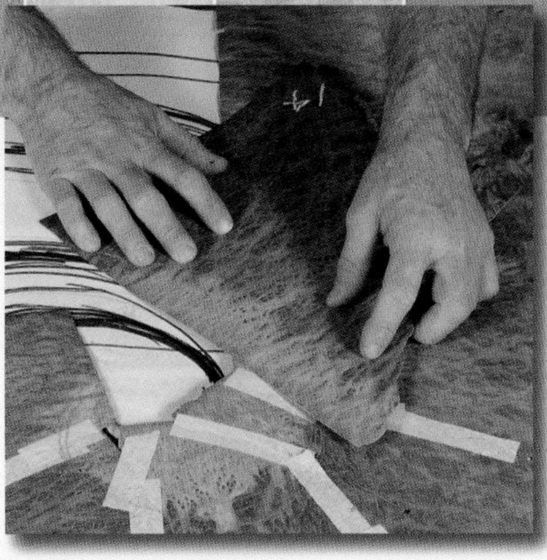

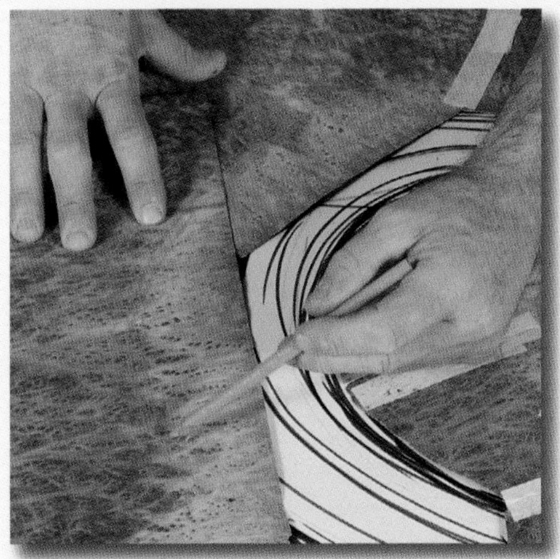

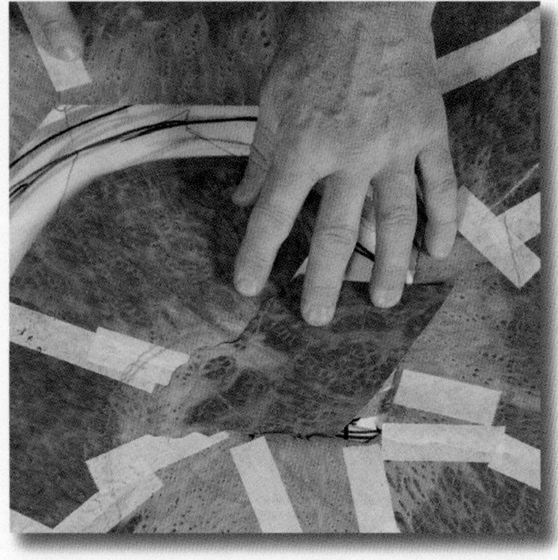

Foreword

Marc Adams

Although working with veneer has been done for thousands of years, it is really just now hitting stride in America—thanks to brilliant craftsmen like Scott Grove. I have been following Scott since the early 1990s and have been impressed by his body of work that includes considerable artistic vigor. His designs are original, expressive, and innovative. In fact he has impacted an entire generation of designers and craftsmen who have incorporated his techniques into their work.

Scott is blessed with technical expertise and has been given the gift of effective communication skills as well. He knows how to guide his understudies through a path of "discovery by directive." With his leadership and instructional sequencing, his students learn hard skills at a fast pace.

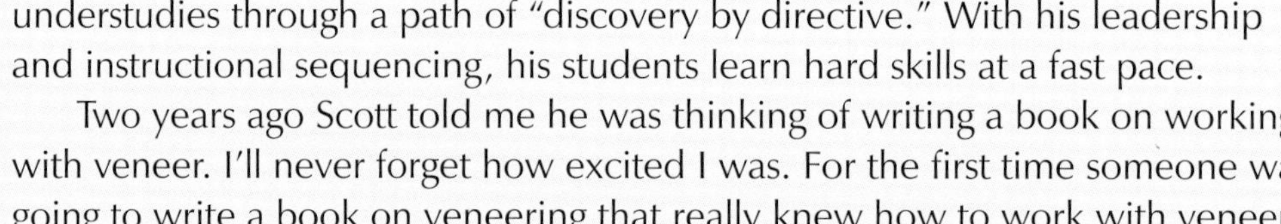

Two years ago Scott told me he was thinking of writing a book on working with veneer. I'll never forget how excited I was. For the first time someone was going to write a book on veneering that really knew how to work with veneer, while at the same time knew how to clearly explain the process.

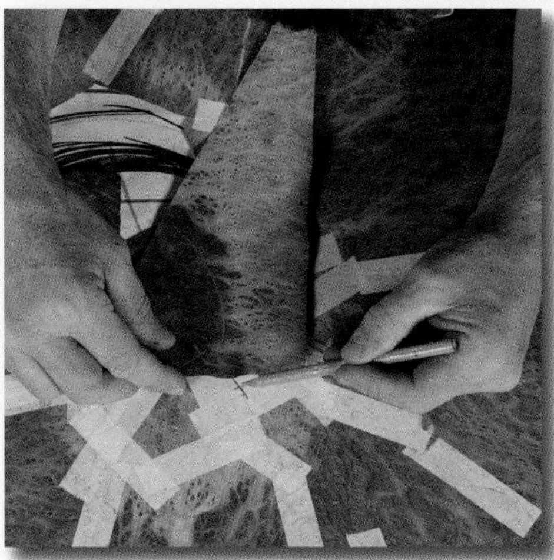

From the first chapter on how veneer is manufactured to the final chapter on wood facts, Scott nailed the essence of the process with insight of years of experience. His layout techniques will help anyone of any skill level do professional work.

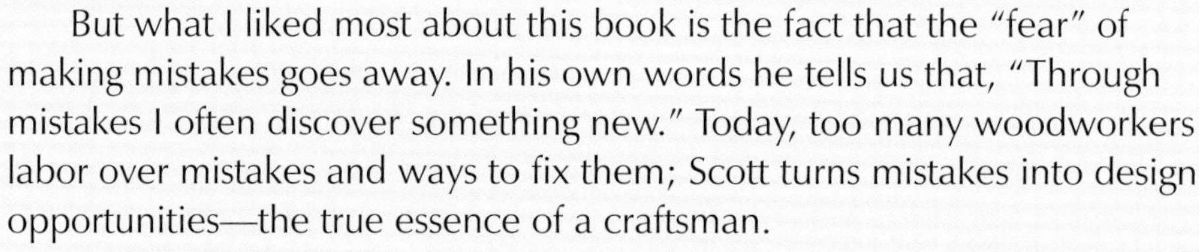

But what I liked most about this book is the fact that the "fear" of making mistakes goes away. In his own words he tells us that, "Through mistakes I often discover something new." Today, too many woodworkers labor over mistakes and ways to fix them; Scott turns mistakes into design opportunities—the true essence of a craftsman.

Scott has taken his craft to a level higher than any other person I have met. He has a creative spirit that is charged with enthusiasm, purpose and passion. What separates Scott from all other woodworking artists/craftsman is how he motivates and inspires us all.

Through his work, teaching abilities, writing skills, modesty, and even the sacrifices he has made, Scott has placed himself on a scale with no equals.

—Marc Adams
Marc Adams School of Woodworking

Introduction

I distinctly remember the first time I recognized and appreciated a piece of highly figured walnut burl veneer. As an impulsive 22-year-old, I bought the old Victorian piano on the spot. It was beautiful, and I was in awe. The imagery within the veneer's figure prompted me to wonder, first, how could anyone improve on Mother Nature's artistic composition? Second, how could anyone work with such a delicate material?

At the time I didn't know anything about collecting antique pianos, nor did I know how to play, but I was so enamored with the craftsmanship and beauty of the wood that I lugged that piano from apartment to apartment for the next ten years.

After my woodworking career was on its way, I was again wowed by highly figured veneer during a visit to Wendell Castle's studio. It was then that I decided to devote the rest of my life to learning everything I could about veneering, and in the process, I developed alternative techniques that improve upon what I perceived as its shortcomings.

I spent many years studying, working, reading and learning everything I could about veneer. A self-taught woodworker, I often learned from observation, persistent questioning, research, and trial and error. Through this self taught discovery, I freed myself from traditional and functionally fixed methods and techniques.

I have had the pleasure of hosting a variety of very talented apprentices and co-op students from the School for American Crafts at RIT (Rochester Institute of Technology) as well as teaching at the Marc Adams School of Woodworking and at many other workshops around the country including MIT, Arizona State University, Savannah College of Art and Design, Sheridan College Institute of Technology - Toronto Canada, and Appalachian State University, to name a few.

Teaching gives me the opportunity to combine, experiment, and test a variety of techniques without the worries of producing a "final piece of art." It allows me to share my knowledge and presents a chance to push the limits, as, in a classroom setting, experimentation is more important than the final product.

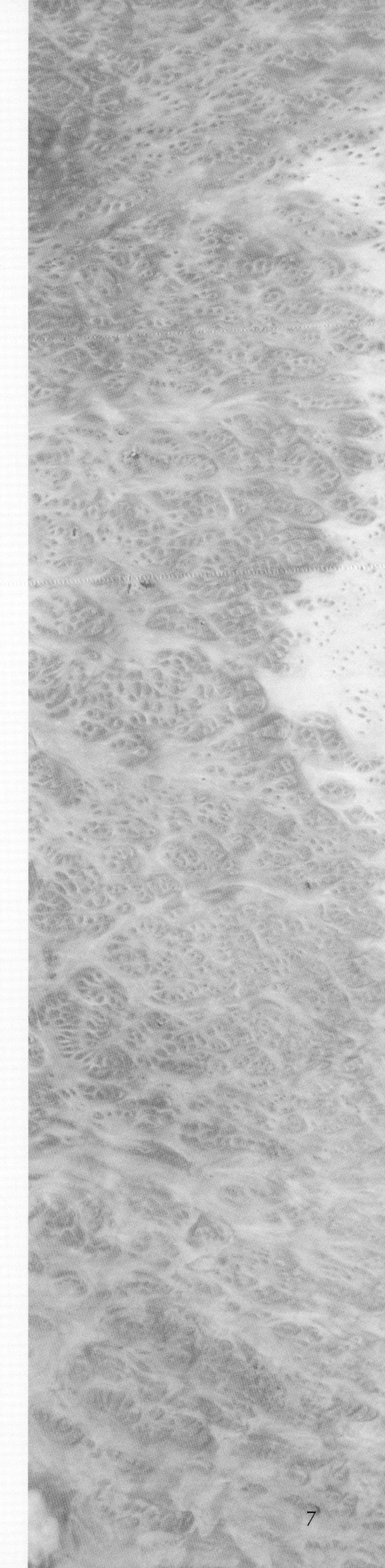

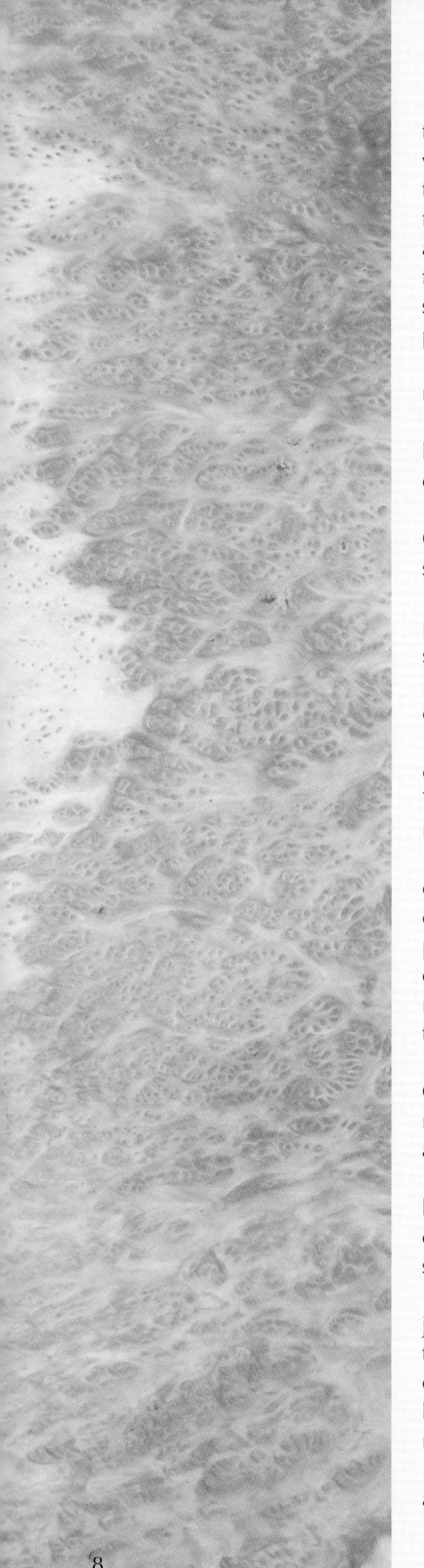

The main focus of this book is alternative and advanced veneering techniques when working with burl veneer. I also review basic terminology as we go along, such as flitch, book matching, platen, etc.; they can be found in the glossary, too. Beginners, hobbyists, students, and experienced craftsmen will find the techniques and information in this book helpful. When approaching a new problem, I like to think of the obvious and then the complete opposite from that perspective. This "devil's advocate" approach can be useful when searching for alternative solutions to standard, complacent, functionally-fixed procedures, and it can also make social conversation quite lively.

Through this experimentation approach I have developed and refined a number of unique techniques that I am proud to share in this book.

The first method is the wavy contour seam in combination with a double bevel cutting technique used to join veneers, best used with burls. It is a cleverly-concealed random curvy seam that squiggles its way through swirling grain.

Traditionally, veneer seams have been performed with a straight seam. Contrary to the swirling grain within a burl, the straight line seam typically stands out, which can detract from the grain's complexity and composition.

This straight seaming is compounded when more complex matching patterns are composed. For example: straight seams are more noticeable in a sunburst pattern (created from a radial match), which intersects in the center. I find this center star of seams very distracting from a beautiful organic bull's eye sunburst of grain.

When concealing a straight seam within the burl's grain using a wavy contour seam, the aesthetic focus shifts from the seam's to the grain's patterns. The wavy contour seam methodology may appear unorthodox at first, but it resolves a fundamental visual conflict.

My second method or approach is asymmetrical matching, specifically called spin and offset matching. Burl veneer is often book matched, which creates a symmetrical pattern (I will cover book matching in Chapter 6). This pattern can be enhanced by incorporating sapwood. Often, sunbursts in a center of the radial match make the best use of these contrasting grains. For me, this matching gets predictable (after all, veneering has been around since the ancient Egyptians, about 5000 years ago).

As a third-generation artist, I prefer to have more creative options. Granted, there are unlimited patterns that can be found in a symmetrical match; nonetheless, symmetry is still predictable. My asymmetrical approach allows for more expressive aesthetic options.

When used in tandem with my wavy contour seam, veneer, particularly burls, can be matched in extremely unique and natural, and unnatural, looking compositions using seams that do not distract from the patterns. These hidden seams and asymmetrical matching opens a new chapter in veneer composition.

Although I admit I am a tool junkie and own many specialty tools, jigs, and dedicated pieces of equipment, I have geared the majority of the techniques in this book toward a woodworker with limited tools and equipment resources. In addition, as my mother always says, "There are a hundred ways to skin a cat," so I show a variety of alterative techniques and methods.

It is important to understand concepts behind a technique's process, although the specific method of execution can be performed in a variety of ways. My fundamental credo is: Whatever works and gets the job done.

I encourage experimentation and pushing the limits. My favorite saying is, "You don't know where the line is until you cross it." Finding and crossing these lines is an important piece of knowledge and fosters a better understanding of the medium, which translates into creative freedom.

And when you've located and crossed your line, figure out how to move it.

For example, how will you know how thin you can make a table leg until one fails and breaks? Or, how much you can sand a veneer table top until you sand through? So, lay up an extra scrap piece, grind it down, and then you'll know.

In respect to a failure, ask yourself: What can be done to fix it? Can it be modified, transformed, and manipulated into an acceptable solution? In these cases, it is important to let go of your expectations; ignore where you were going and see instead where it might take you.

Through mistakes I often discover something new: a new aesthetic or possible new technique. For example, after many hours of working on an executive desk with a beautiful piece of veneer and maple hardwood edge, the edge received a horrific knife cut perpendicular to the grain. It was too deep to sand out and was essentially un-repairable.

My solution was to cut into the deep score with my dovetail saw, cutting all the way through the hardwood edge right into the veneer field, and then I filled the kerf with a sliver of black veneer. The result resembled a hash mark on a numberless clock.

I liked this so much I ended up cutting lines all the way around the table top. This also led to cutting into all my hardwood butt seams, covering up one of the slightly less-than-perfect seams in the process.

So, my one mistake spawned a new aesthetic (the black hash marks) and an alternative solution to "questionable" butt seams. Please keep the adage in mind: There is no such thing as a mistake, only an opportunity to push the line forward.

In this book not all the technique examples are sequenced with the same project, as I repeat many of them and use the best photographic examples I could find. I review some veneering fundamentals, along with alternatives, tips, and advanced techniques.

I worked with a number of species of wood on different projects while photographing this book and you will see a variety of them as examples. There is something for everyone.

Lastly, our planet relies on the health of one of its largest natural living renewable resources: trees. It's important that we, especially as woodworkers, are aware of our impact on the natural world.

As an integral part of this shared ecological community, it is our duty to consume responsibly, and luckily for us, using veneer is, in itself, a green process. Veneers are obtained from sustainable woods that offer a higher grade in figure (bird's eye, quilting) while yielding 42 times more surface area than standard hardwood. That means we can be sensitive to our environmental impact while using this material to make incredibly beautiful artful objects.

I hope you enjoy.

—Scott Grove

TIP: Always lay up an extra piece of veneer on every project for testing.

1
Veneer Milling

Veneer, according to Mirriam-Webster, is "a thin sheet of a material as a) a layer of wood of superior value or excellent grain to be glued to an inferior wood; b) any of the thin layers bonded together to form plywood; c) a plastic or porcelain coating bonded to the surface of a cosmetically imperfect tooth." (I wonder what wood was used for George Washington's dentures.)

Specific to wood, veneer is generally 1/42 of an inch thick (.024"), varying depending on the species of wood, the veneer processor, or level of technology being used. It seems that "they" keep trying to get more slices out of an inch of wood every year. Some veneers are now as thin as 1/100 of an inch. In my opinion, this is just too thin for us woodworkers to handle and is best left to cheap production furniture makers.

Bad Rap

During the Renaissance (roughly 14th -17th centuries), veneering was considered one of the highest art forms. Many of these works of art are still around today, accompanied by high price tags.

The fact is, veneer is typically the highest quality wood with respect to consistency in figure, grain, and color. When a quality tree or burl is discovered (yes, they are "discovered" as the grain quality can not be seen until the tree is cut), it is often shipped to veneer plants, as it commands a higher price.

Because veneer maximizes a tree's harvest and has such a high yield, using it makes ecological sense. It also allows for far more visual options than hardwood. A craftsman can separate structural aspects and focus on the aesthetic composition when overlaying veneer onto a structural substrate.

This brings me to the 20th century perception of veneer as being cheap or of lesser quality than solid hardwood. The stigma of "cheap" is due to the development, in the early 1960s, of poorly engineered substrates made with inferior adhesives such as particle board, which resulted in major failures.

Since then, great strides have been made, and engineered substrates are now far superior to their predecessors. They are time-tested and will last for generations to come. Welcome to the 21st century.

Making Veneer

From ancient times until the last century, veneer was sawn, leaving a kerf (a void created by the cutting saw blade) which was extremely wasteful and time consuming.

Since then the process has been refined to slicing (not cutting) and is a reasonably simple process: Find a really nice looking piece of lumber. Boil it in water until the wood becomes soft. Slice the hunk into very thin sheets. Keep all the leaves in order and dry them flat. Trim off the waste, sort, bundle, and sell.

This sounds simple enough, but seeing this in action is another thing altogether. Luckily I had a wonderful opportunity to get an exclusive tour by Mike Maier, vice president of operations of the Danzer Specialty Veneers mill, formerly David R. Webb Company in Edinburgh, Indiana.

The Danzer mill is one of the largest veneer plants in the United States and is part of the largest veneer processing conglomerates in the world. It is a *very* impressive operation.

Brief history: Back in the 1800s when the Appalachian region was developing its lumber production capabilities, the industry needed a flat area close to river-based transportation. For a variety of reasons, Edinburgh became our nation's epicenter of lumber milling, which later evolved into veneer milling.

Logs and burls are harvested from a variety of sources, from large company-owned forests to independent one-man logging operations. Prices vary as with any commodity; they have steadily increased over the last ten years, and are projected to continue to increase (yet another reason to use veneer).

Although each veneer mill has its own proprietary techniques, equipment, and formulations, the general process has been the same for centuries.

Burls are typically found on the root system and can also attach to a branch or tree trunk. They are caused by environmental stress such as insects, mold infestation or early growth structural damage. They can also be induced by man.

A burl is a bulbous growth, a type of malignancy which drastically deforms the grain, making it highly figured, unusual and more valuable. *Photo courtesy of Certainly Wood.*

The following images show step-by-step veneer milling. The day I toured the plant they were not slicing burls, although the process is similar.

You never know what you're going to get…until the bark is removed. Here a maple log reveals a nice figure with shimmering curls perpendicular to the length of the tree. This will yield curly maple veneer.

Logs are sorted by species and graded for a variety of characteristics such as straightness, figure (after a section of bark is removed), and size. This mill can process 30,000 board feet of wood per day, which turns into roughly 200,000 square meters of veneer or 1.8 million square feet.

The average log size ranges from 14″ to 32″ diameter, depending on the species. This large old growth fir could be 100+ years in age. The largest Douglas fir cut at this plant has been 60″ in diameter.

Old growth lumber is becoming very scarce; salvaging it from beneath our water systems and from architectural structures such as barns and factories is now becoming a viable resource.

Logs are cut into lengths from 6 to 12 feet in order to obtain the straightest log possible that will, in turn, yield more veneer.

The logs are loaded onto a huge geared conveyor. The next step is "stumping," which helps make the log more cylindrical. This process grinds the bottom end of the log where it flares out and turns it into a stump. Note: All the machinery at this plant is massive and runs at blinding speed.

The logs are de-barked with two different cutting heads: course and fine. As the debarked logs move down the conveyor, they are scanned through two metal detectors for nails and the like (see orange octagonal frames in background). If metal is detected, the trees are culled out and hand-scanned for removal of the iron debris. Burls are all power washed by hand, scanned, and visually inspected with care for stones or other knife-damaging debris.

For initial rough slab cutting, the log is grabbed by a large set of tongs mounted on a fast moving carriage. An operator uses a laser to align the log to a huge band saw with a blade that is 12″ wide by 44″ long. The log is cut in half lengthwise. For the first cut, a minimal slab is faced off (enough for a reference surface for future milling operations), then a center cut is made. The third cut is the opposing face, which is similar to the first cut. The carriage glides back and forth at incredible speed, all controlled by a skilled operator working a joystick that would give my two video-playing sons a run for their money.

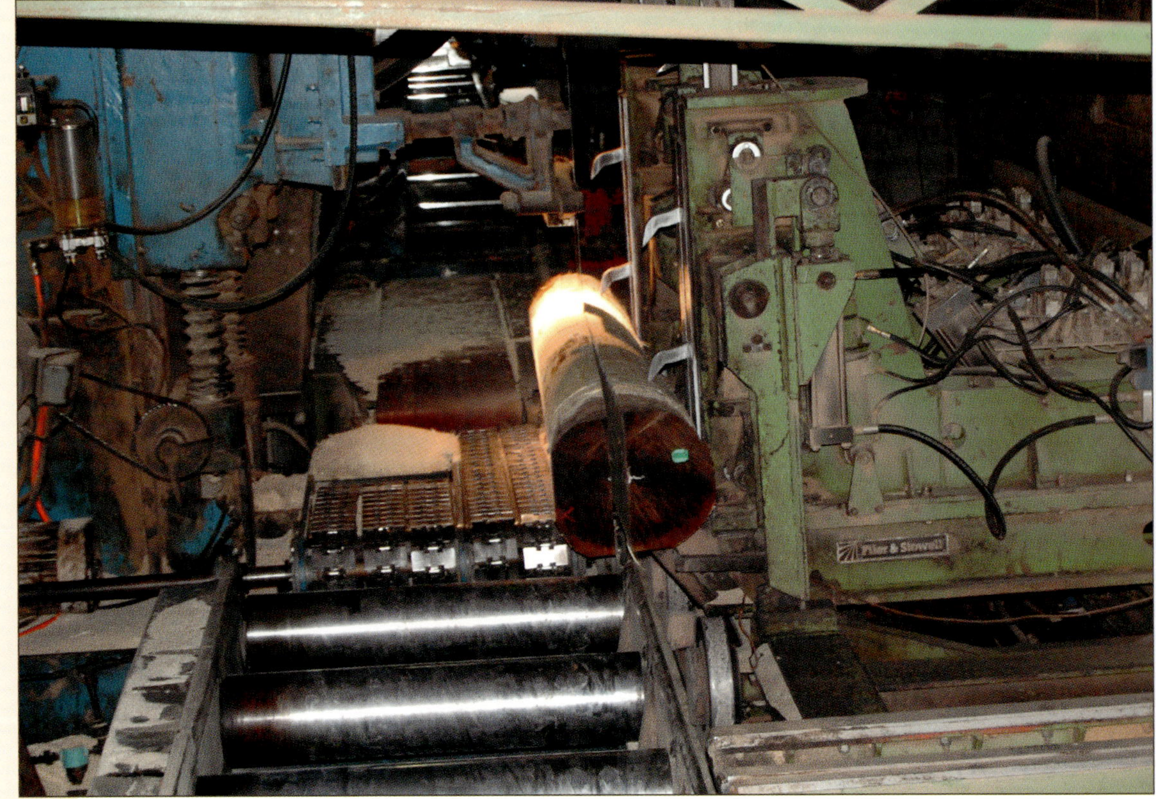

The two log halves are banded together, bundled with additional pairs of logs by species, and soaked or boiled in 21,000 gallon cooking vats that hold up to 8,000 board feet (BF) of lumber in each vat.

Banks of soaking vats that are accessed by an overhead crane. In a clever case of recycling, wood chips from the milling process fuel the heating boilers. Depending on the species and size of the wood blanks, the lumber will soak for one to four days, from room temperature to 120 degrees Fahrenheit. This process softens the lignum in the wood, which is the natural tree resin or glue that holds the wood fibers together. This softening process allows the wood to be milled more easily and the veneer can be thinly sliced without splitting or cracking.

The log ends are trimmed, then the reference face is joined flat and opposing faces are planed parallel.

NOTE: The slicing process does not produce a kerf (a void created by a saw blade), hence, there is minimal waste. Any leftovers are used to heat the plant and its softening vats.

Types of Slicing

Veneer is most commonly sliced one of three ways: plane, quartered, or rotary.

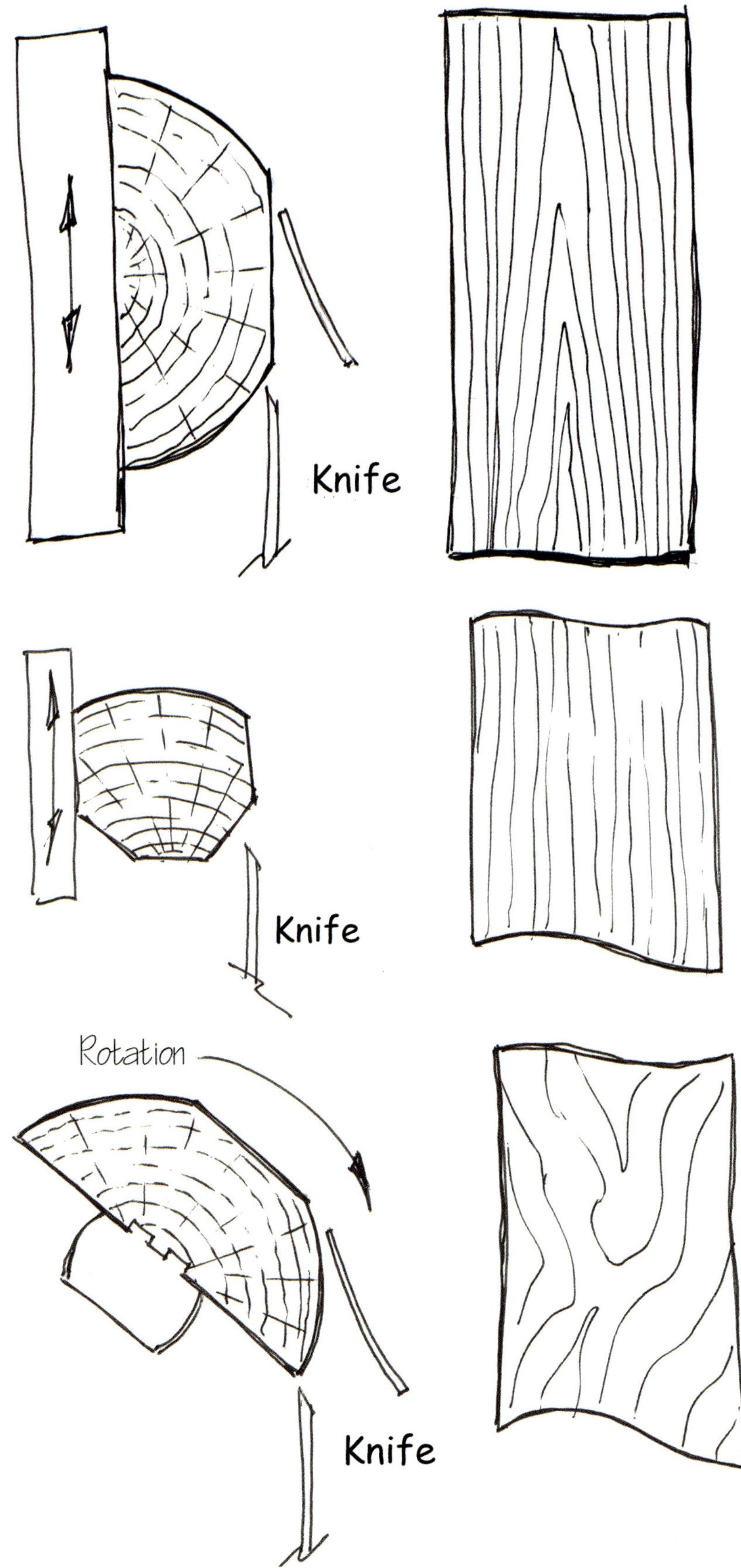

A **PLANE SLICE** yields a cathedral grain pattern in the center and straight quarter grain pattern at the edges.

A **QUARTER CUT** produces narrower leaves with a straight grain pattern. Since the cut is perpendicular to the grain it also reveals median rays that can produce flecks and shimmering grain patterns.

A **ROTARY CUT** typically yields the widest leaves and is most often used with burls. The grain is most random in pattern.

The two grooves cut into the reference face are used to clamp the blank to the lathe for rotary cutting. These grooves are milled in during the joining and planing steps. See bottom image on page 15.

If the veneer is to be rotary cut (a type of veneer slicing), additional clamping grooves are also milled into the reference face. All this is controlled by bar codes that follow the log through the entire process.

This huge lathe is used for rotary slicing; a 12-foot slicing blade steps in at each rotation. Veneer is typically cut at 1/42 of an inch thickness. Simply stated, veneer will yield 42 times more surface area than solid hardwood.

A log is being loaded onto the cutting platen and held into place by vacuum *only*. For plain and quarter slicing the log is moved up and down vertically across the knife.

Maple burl mounted on a lathe slicer for rotary cutting.

The veneer leaves peel off and are constantly inspected.

Leaves are randomly culled for closer inspection to help establish the quality of the cut and determine if a knife requires sharpening.

The leaves immediately go into a dryer, moving up and down a 220 foot beltway of drying screens that keep the veneer flat during drying.

Once dried to a moisture content of 6% to 9%, the leaves are carefully stacked in sequence, typically in bundles or packs of 24 leaves. Each veneer pack has a bar code with pertinent information such as original log, source, species and a sequenced identification number.

Veneer packs are stored as complete logs or flitches.

The packs are inspected, preliminarily graded and trimmed for better veneer value. For example, the edges of a plane-sliced log may have a figured grain toward the edges; this higher-value veneer will be trimmed off, packaged and sold separately. (See rendering, top of page 20.)

The trimmed packs are labeled, bundled, and stacked for final grading.

Each pack is individually inspected for the last time and categorized in up to 25 different grades. Each manufacturer has their own grading system. Grading is subjective and can change along the distribution chain.

The graded veneer packs are stacked in sequence, each with an identifying label and bar code, which allows distributors to trace the veneer back to its origins.

2
Purchasing & Inspecting

Purchasing

When buying veneer, especially burl, selecting just the right one for the best visual impact can be tedious. Within one species, and even within the same burl, grain patterns can change drastically. Obviously it is best to see the veneer in person before purchasing, but is not often possible.

Understanding grain terminology such as sapwood, curl, blister, flame, chatoyance, muscle, and the like will help you communicate with the salesperson (see Appendix B for definitions). Many suppliers have websites with images and/or can send you digital photos of specific leaves. When placing large orders, veneer vendors can also send you samples.

Often leaves may come "clipped" (edges trimmed so they are straighter). It is important to know if the veneer is not clipped when ordering, since the width may drastically vary from end to end, which affects the maximum width yield.

Veneer is usually packaged in bundles of 24 leaves (some imports may be 32 leaves) and crated in a "flitch," which can be half the log or the entire log. These leaves are sequenced in the order from which they were cut off the log or burl. Flitches are crated; bundles are either shipped in crates, rolled in boxes, or placed flat between thick cardboard. Burls are usually shipped flat due to their brittleness.

Inspecting

The first leaf in each bundle typically has a label identifying pertinent information such as when it was cut, a sequence number, and additional information. Keep these numbers handy in case you want to order more, so you can hopefully get the next set of consecutive leaves for a consistent figure. If you are only buying one or two leaves, request these numbers for the same reasons.

The first thing I do when receiving a large order is to check for "leaf shift" (see page 26). To do this, check a dominant grain pattern such as a knot and its relationship to an edge. If this spot moves more than a half of an inch, this could be "leaf shift" that may affect your material yield during the layout and matching steps. This is a rare occurrence, but it can cause all sorts of alignment and yield problems.

THE FIRST STEP: label each leaf in order to keep track of the sequence. Note: If you plan to flatten the veneer, use an oil-based pencil on the corner, as chalk will wash off. Or be very careful and keep the leaves in order when flattening.

Inspect each sheet or leaf for defects such as cracks, checks, voids, and missing or broken areas that will need to be repaired. This mappa burl has all three.

Temporarily tape these defects, especially the cracks, as well as the entire perimeter, with light-tack masking tape to keep them from getting worse. Once you have determined which side of the veneer will be facing up as shown, you can protect these damaged areas more securely with veneer tape. See Chapter 8, Taping, page 100.

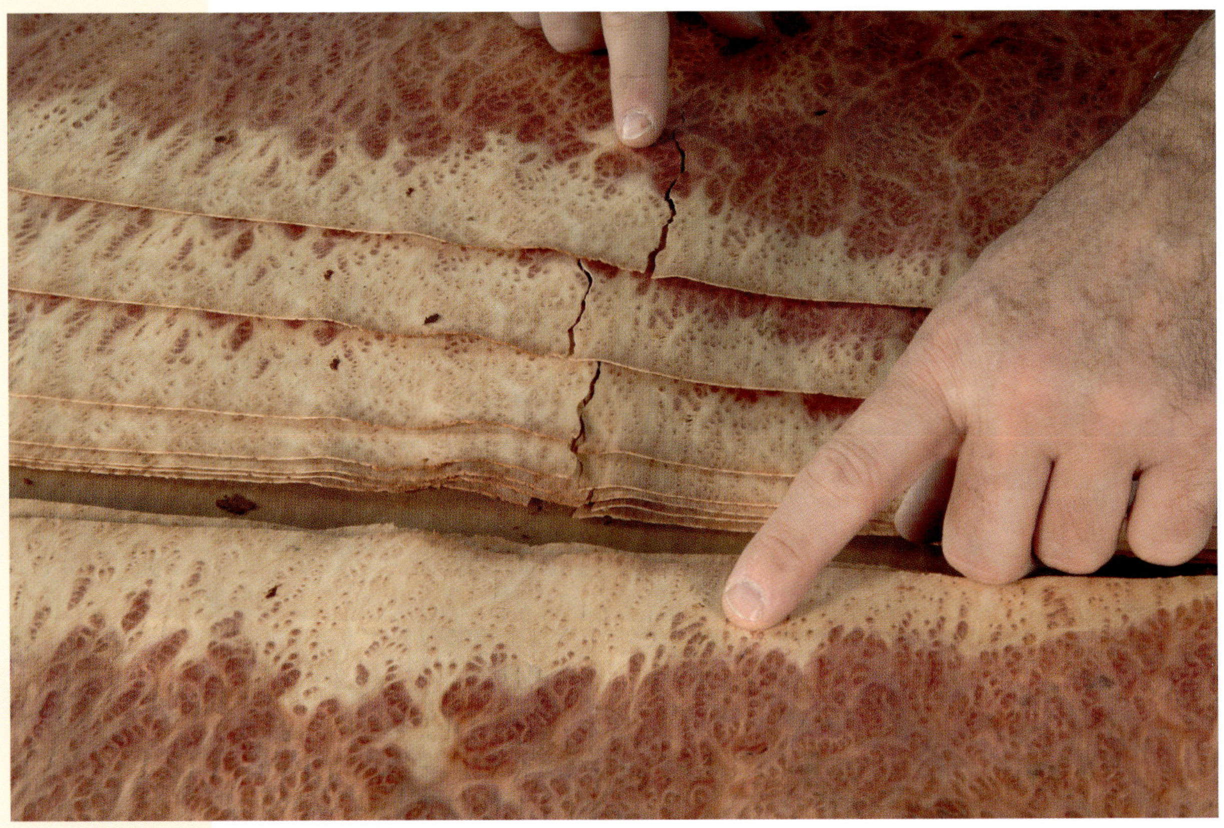

Be sure to carefully inspect every leaf of veneer as defects appear within a few pieces from the start of the bundle.

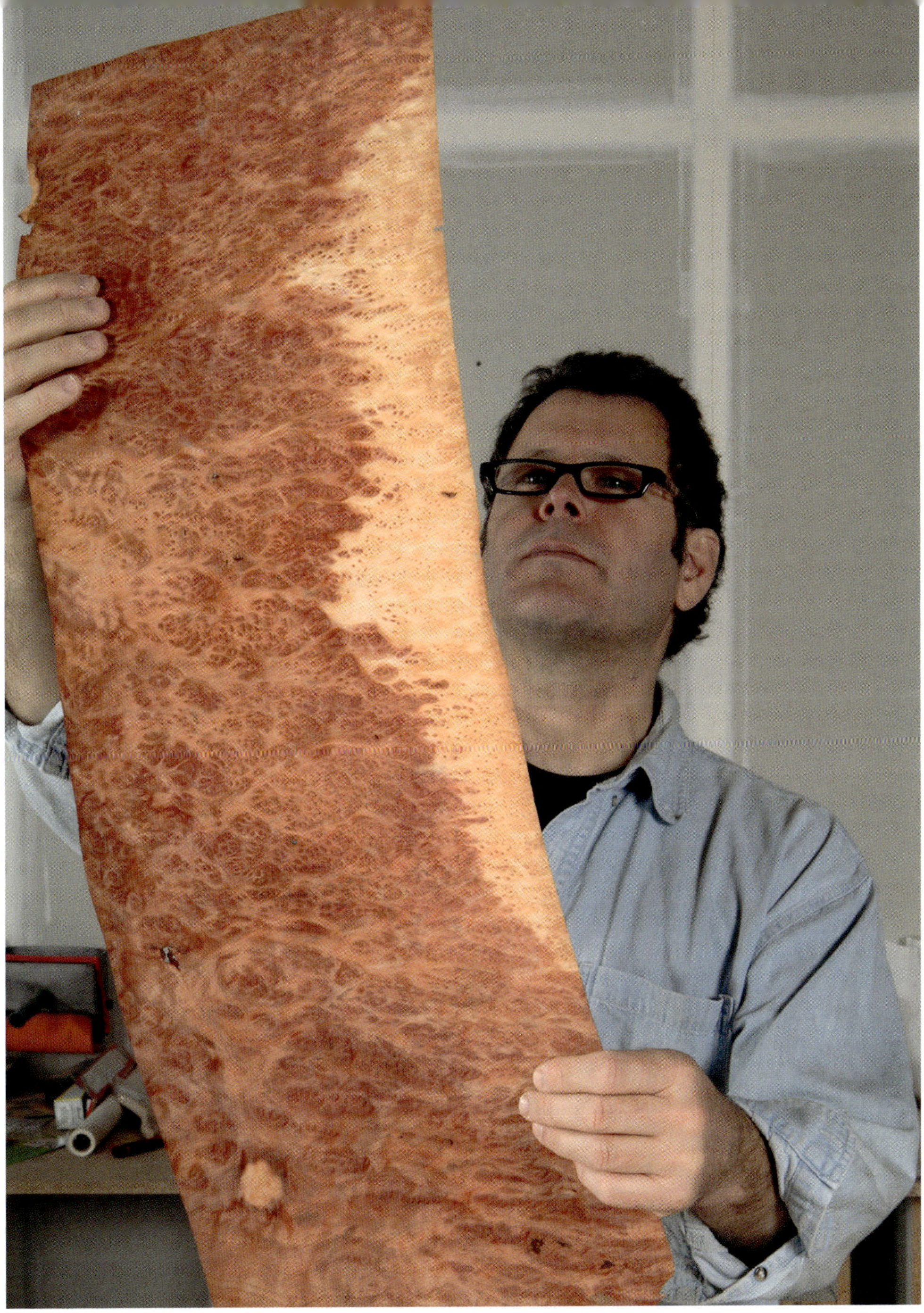

Look for "shim sheets" or leaves that are extra thin due to a skip in the slicing process. Hold each leaf up to a light to easily identify thin areas. Save these sheets to use for possible repairs.

Sometimes you will find embedded veneer chips that have left a deep impression. This leaf's impression will need to be repaired or avoided during the layout process. The indent can be either repaired with an iron by steaming and swelling the wood out to a consistent thickness, or by filling it in during the finishing process. See Chapter 4, Repairs, page 34.

Although the figure will gradually change from leaf to leaf (called grain drift), some figures may drastically move (called leaf shift) offsetting the grain pattern drastically.

Grain drifts naturally from leaf to leaf.

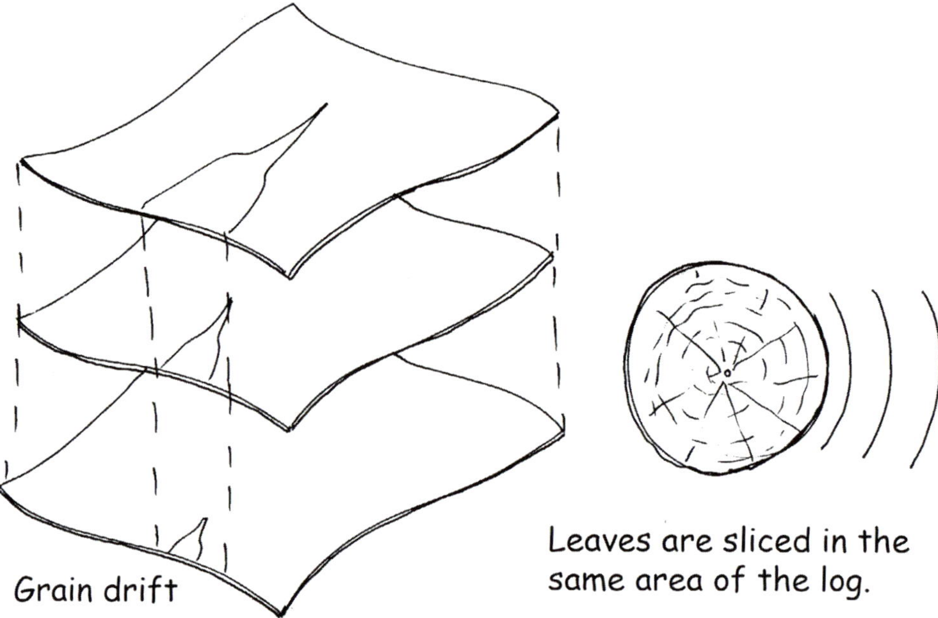

Leaf shift happens when the veneer leaves are removed from different areas of the log, causing the grain to significantly shift relative to its location on each leaf.

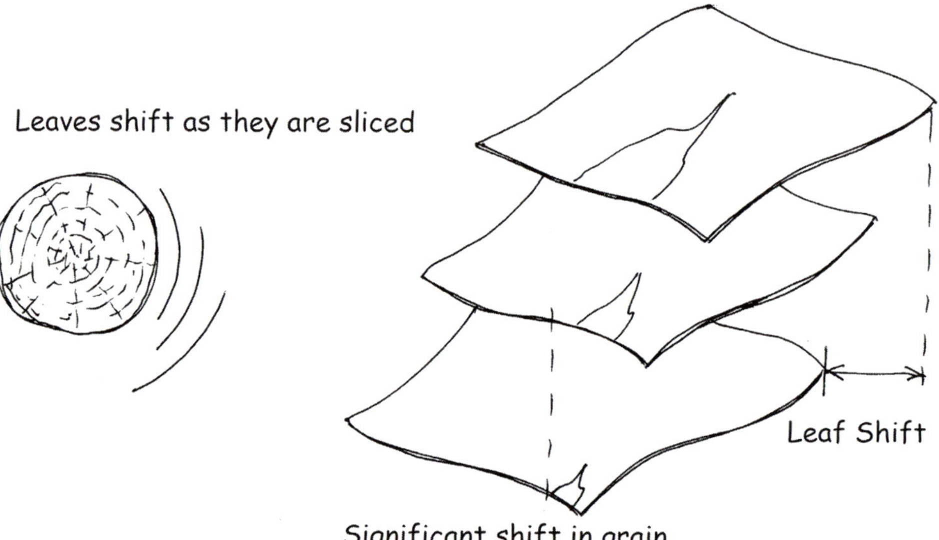

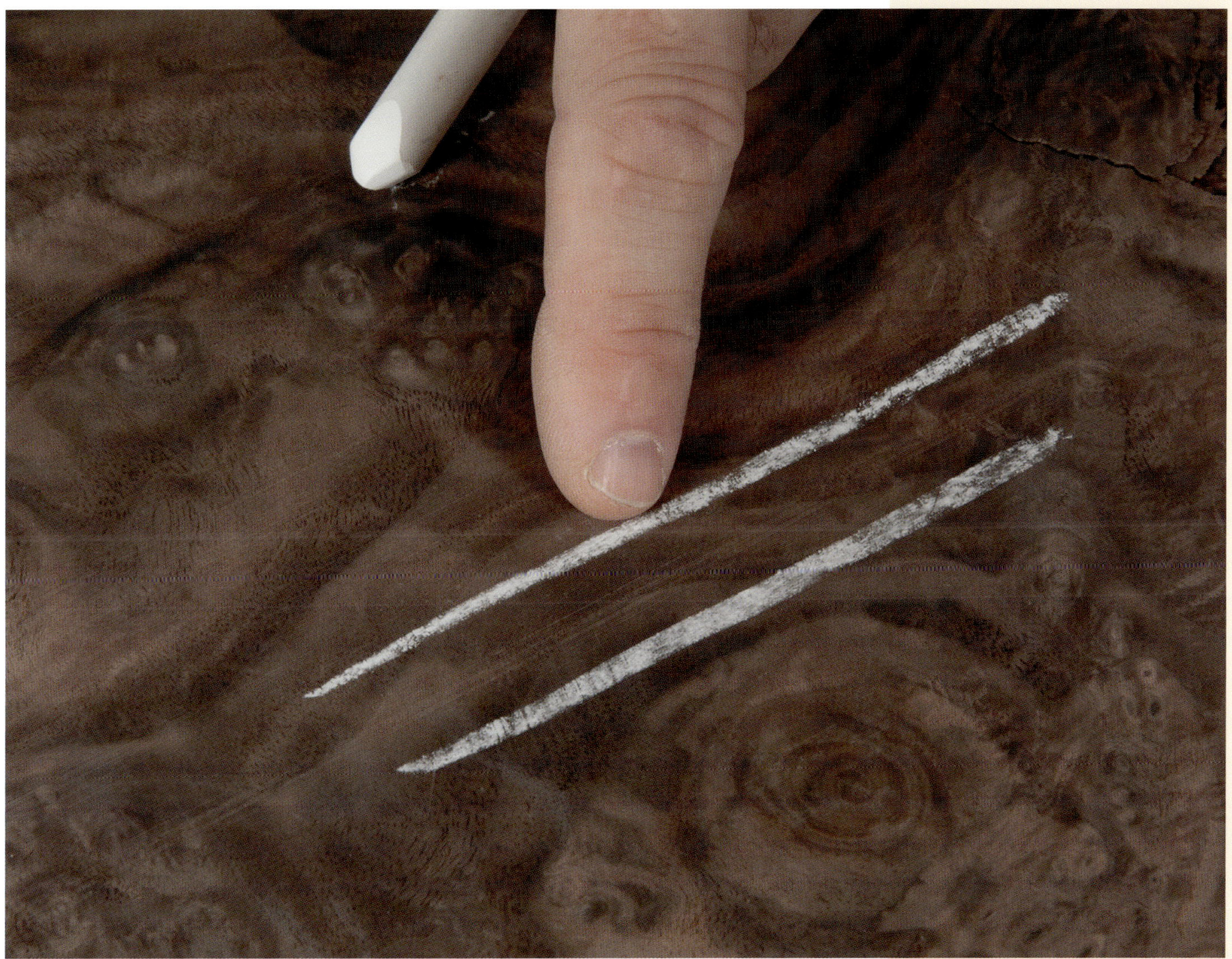

Look for surface scars or scratches from nicks in the slicing knife. These scrapes will appear to be a depression or a valley on one side of the leaf and a bump or peak on the other side. These can sometimes be steamed out as stated above, but they often have to be sanded out.

Other surface defects to look for are surface checks, or small cracks typically found on one side of the leaf. These will give you insight on identifying the compression and stretched (checked) side of the veneer.

As veneer is sliced, it curls away from the log, stretching that face of veneer which can create tiny checks; the other side is compressed. These different sides can affect a number of issues such as how the veneer reflects light (its chatoyance), absorbs glue, and shows the checks (more on this in other Chapters).

Sometimes it is impossible to identify which side is which and most often it doesn't matter, as both sides will be facing up, as in a book match.

3 Flattening & Conditioning Veneer

Burls inherently contain internal stress due to the swirling grain. Many are gnarly and buckled, and gluing these flat to a board often result in splitting and cracking, and if you're seaming the veneer together, the process can be unworkable.

In addition, some species may be inherently dry and brittle, which makes cutting them without chipping almost impossible. In both of these cases, flattening (or conditioning) the veneer is the only way to go.

Flattening softens the wood fibers, making the veneer more pliable and easier to work with. Only experience and working by feel will give you a sense of what is acceptable and when flattening is required.

A good rule of thumb is: if the surface varies more than .25" in height over an inch width, it is best to flatten the veneer. I also flex the veneer between my thumb, first and middle finger to determine its brittleness. If the veneer cracks with moderate pressure, conditioning will help.

There are a number of very good commercial flattening agents on the market that are proven to work and are consistent in their formulation. The veneer may require a hot press to thoroughly dry out the commercial solution during the flattening and/or glue pressing process. Some commercial softeners will allow the veneer to dry out over time and become brittle again, and some may affect veneer adhesion if you are cold pressing with PVA glues, so testing is strongly recommended.

DIY Home Brew

This home brew formulation has an advantage over some commercial softeners, as the glue adds structural integrity to the veneer, essentially gluing the veneer fibers flat.

I have tested variations and use my home brew in an assortment of applications and ratios many times (with the help of my students) and my conclusion is that the exact ratio is not critical. I have even completely eliminated each of the parts one at a time (except the water) and still have had success.

My starting formula is as follows:

- 3 parts water
- 2 parts PVA glue – poly vinyl acetate
- 1 part glycerin
- 1/2 part alcohol
- 1/2 part acetone

Dissolve the glycerin into the alcohol first, then add the acetone, then the water, and finally, the glue. The bottom line is that if the glycerin is added last to the mixture, it will congeal and not blend in.

TIP: Mix one quart of total mixture for every ten square feet of veneer to be flattened. This will vary depending on the species and dryness of wood.

I prefer a home brew made of readily-available ingredients that is easy to use; I have used the formulation above for many years with great results, and it has a long shelf life.

TIP: Glycerin can be purchase in small quantities at most pharmacies or in bulk at Farm & Feed Stores or online.

The flattening process is as follows:

Liberally brush the solution on both sides of the veneer, stacking the wet veneer on itself as you go along. Keep the leaves wet, in sequence, and in the same orientation.

Wrap all the pieces together in plastic and let the brew absorb into the veneer for about 10 to 30 minutes. The veneer can sit longer, even overnight, as long as it doesn't dry out.

I like to mark the time on the plastic, as I often lose track of it while I'm in the "shop zone," a good practice for many of the next steps that are time sensitive.

Unwrap the veneer and wipe off any excess surface solution using plenty of paper towels, or a sponge. You may skip this step and proceed to the next "air dry" step if you don't want to waste all the paper towels. The objective of the following steps is to remove all the moisture; wiping quickens the process.

After the veneer has thoroughly absorbed the flattening solution, the wood will be very pliable.

Hang the leaves individually so they can air dry and remove the balance of the *surface* moisture. The drying time depends on the amount of solution left on the surface, the species of wood, ambient temperature, relatively humidity, and air movement. It can take from 15 minutes to two hours to air dry. Note the glossy wet surface sheen.

The goal is to evaporate the majority of the solution off the *surface*. It is not an exact science; when the glossy sheen is gone from the surface, you're ready to move on to the flattening process. It is okay if you don't evaporate all the moisture off the surface (leaving some shininess), as the next steps continue to remove moisture. Be sure not to let the veneer completely dry out.

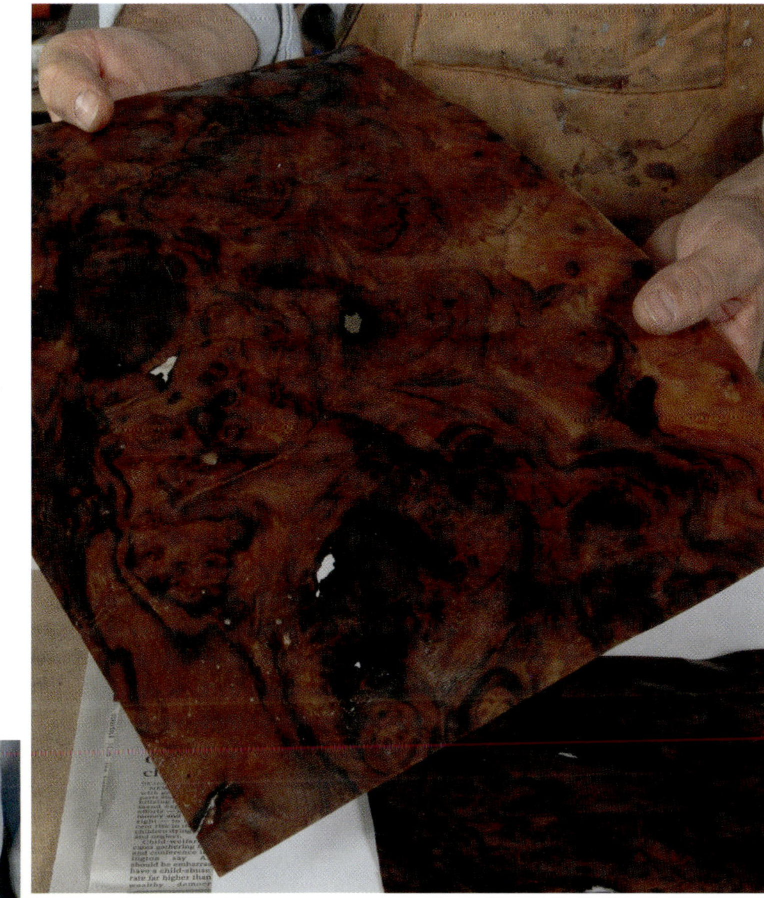

Stack each leaf between a few sheets of white paper, alternating between veneer and paper (this process will be repeated a number of times, so have plenty of paper on hand). The paper will absorb the moisture from here on out.

For the first round of flattening, I prefer to use clean, white newsprint for *direct* contact to the veneer. Regular newsprint ink can stain the veneer.

TIP: Local newspaper printers will often give away or sell end rolls of blank newsprint paper at a reasonable price.

The paper should be left in contact with the veneer only for a **very short period of time**: a quick in and out will work. This step is risky, as it is intended absorb the moisture quicker with direct contact to the paper.

If you use printed newspaper, you risk transferring the ink to the veneer (hence the white paper for direct contact). If you can not monitor your time effectively, skip this step and proceed to the next. Write down your time as you did on the plastic earlier in the flattening process.

If you glue the paper to the veneer, the paper can be removed with a scraper, only if caught early while the paper is still moist. Do this right away before the paper has a chance to dry and completely stick to the veneer. Adding more flattening solution will help loosen the paper, but you'll essentially have to start the flattening process over.

Top:
Place the stack between two cauls (.75" or thicker boards of plywood, chip board, MDF or the like) that are slightly oversized from the veneer leaves and slowly press the sheets flat by hand.

Bottom:
Place weight on the platens. I use three or four 50-pound sand bags. For larger leaves, I break out my vacuum press to flatten. Note: In a vacuum, the moisture can't *evaporate* and you are relying on the paper only to *absorb* the moisture. Pressing in a screw press or with clamps will also work but is not necessary and takes more time.

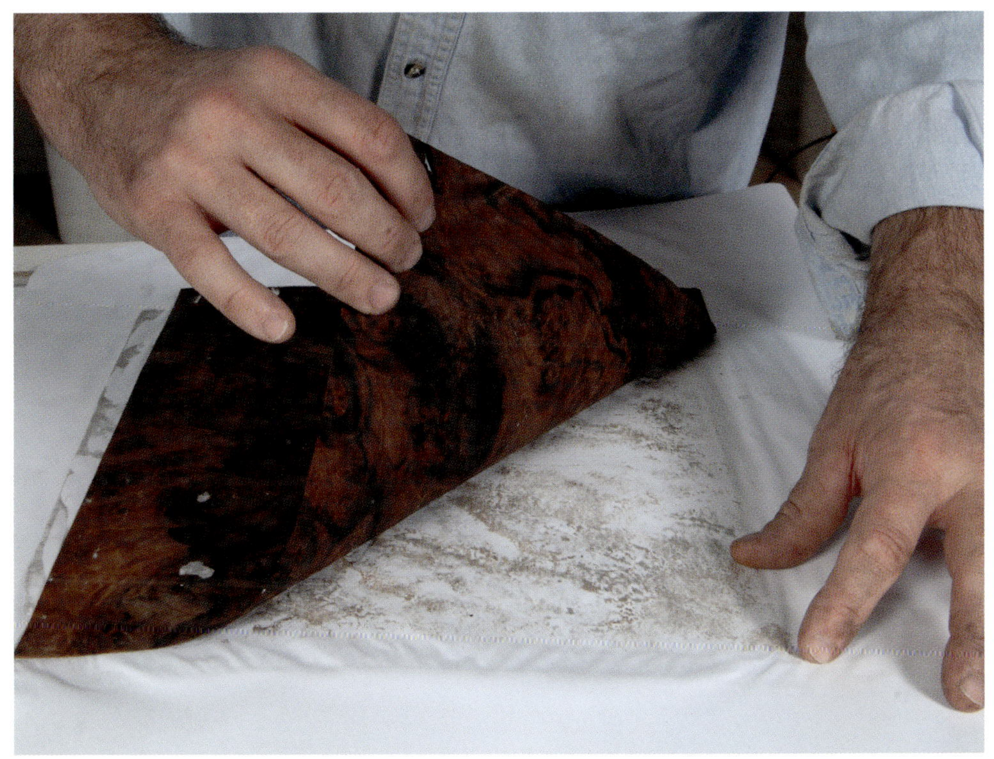

After ***ONLY*** five minutes, remove the weight (or remove from vacuum bag) and discard the paper.

Warning: Many woodworkers recommend not stacking the veneer directly in contact with the paper, as it may glue the paper to the veneer. **This is true**…if the stack is left too long under pressure. Be warned. This photo shows the paper starting to stick as well as transferring ink.

TIP: Glossy paper is not as absorbent as matte.

The time it takes for the second round of pressing depends on a variety of factors such as temperature, relative humidity, and the type of pressing (open air pressing versus a vacuum press or hot press).

The pressing time is not critical as the fiberglass screening will prevent the paper from sticking to the veneer. Generally one hour is good.

Repeat this process three or five more times, changing the paper each time until the veneer is dry. The pressing time is extended at each change of paper. You will notice the paper becoming less moist after each changing. This will be one of your gauges of when to stop. This is a "by feel" type of process and the number of paper changes varies.

On the final pressing, I do two new things. First, after pulling out the paper, I lay the veneer leaves out on a table for five minutes to set any remaining surface glue. Then I restack the veneer without the fiberglass screening in between; the veneer should be dry enough so it will not glue itself to the paper. I let this pressing sit overnight.

Next, sandwich the individual leaves between fiberglass window screening.

Stack the screen with veneer between a few sheets of newspaper. The veneer should not be in contact with the paper. The sequence is: paper, screen, veneer, screen, paper, screen, veneer, screen, paper, and so on.

Restack between the cauls.

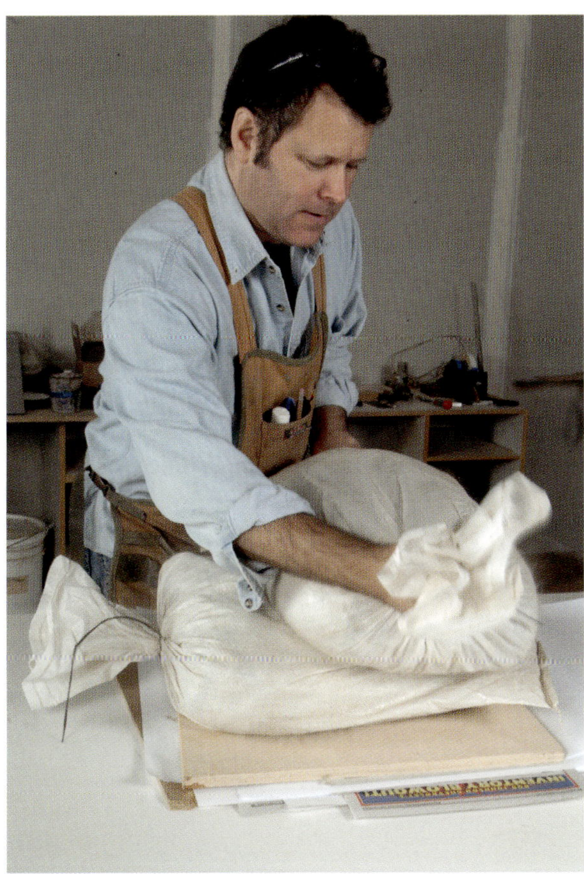

Apply weight (or vacuum) as before.

The following sequence and accelerated tricks let me get the entire process done in 24 hours:

My schedule is:

- Soak veneer in solution wrapped in plastic: 30 minutes.
- Wipe dry / hang: 15 - 120 minutes.
- First press direct white paper contact: 5 minutes.
- Second press with fiberglass screening: one hour.
- Third press with fiberglass screening: three hours.
- Fourth press if paper is still damp: three hours.
- Pull veneer, let air dry: five minutes.
- Final press: press direct contact to paper, overnight, no screening.

Repeat this process three to five times.

The final flattened veneer will feel like leather; it will be dead flat and very pliable. If stored flat between two pieces of plywood or stiff cardboard, it will remain flat. Its pliability will slowly fade but it will always have more integrity than its original state because the home brew essentially glues the fibers flat.

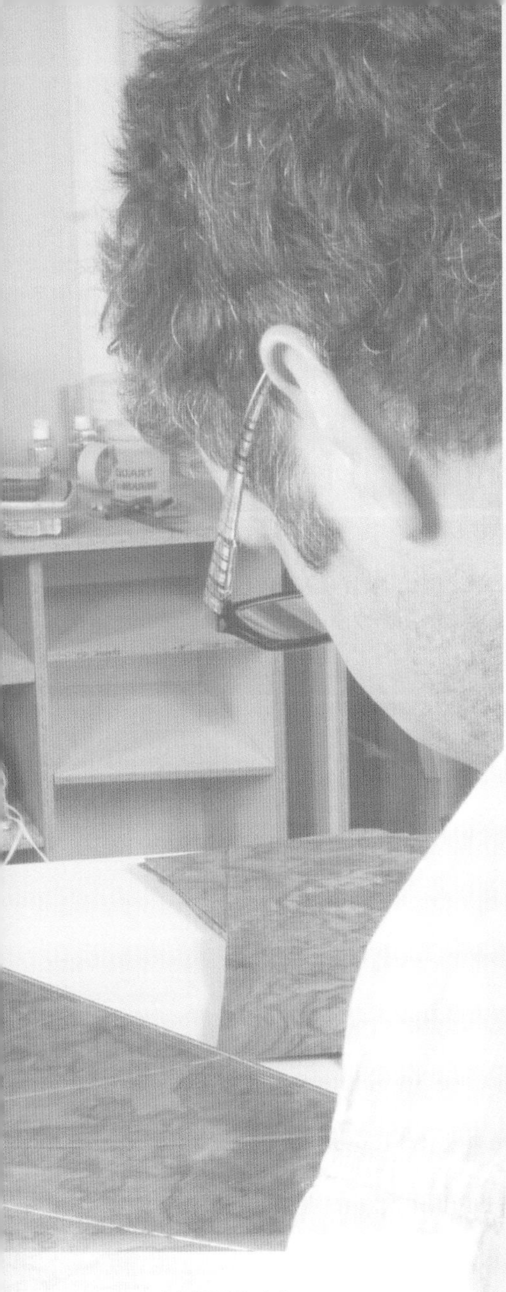

NOTE: Veneer tape is applied only to the face-up side and should never, under any circumstances, be left in the glue line between the veneer and gluing substrate.
See Chapter 8 - Taping

4
Repairs

Repairing veneer is inevitable, especially when working with burls. Burl repairs are very easy to do and, more importantly, to hide. Determining what to repair and at what stage of the handling, pressing, or finishing depends on a variety of factors such as the severity, size, type, and location of the damage.

For example:

Small knot holes and fissures can be repaired easily during the final finishing process.

Dents can be steamed out before or after pressing to a substrate.

Cracks should be temporarily seamed together with removable masking tape (i.e. blue painter's tape) during the initial inspection to avoid any further damage, and then securely taped face-up before pressing.

Larger voids should be repaired after the layout and face-side up is determined, and before gluing to the substrate. These larger repairs can be performed with a variety of techniques using different sized punches, hand inlays, and/or large patches as described below.

Plug cutters are quick and easy to use for moderate sized repairs. Depending on the species of wood, tool sharpness, and If the veneer has been flattened, the cut may not be clean. The veneer patch edge can be lightly hand sanded to clean up any rough spots.

For repairs that are too large for a plug cutter, use a hand fret or power scroll saw to create a double-bevel inlay cut (see top illustration on page 48).

For large patches, it is more important to match the veneer color and value (the lightness or darkness of the wood) than matching the grain. The grain can be easily painted in during the touch up and finishing process (see bottom image on page 67).

To start, wipe a little mineral spirits or naphtha (paint thinner) on the veneer to give you a truer color rendition of what it will look like after clear finishing.

Small knot holes are repaired during the final finishing. See Chapter 4, Repair, page 63.

NOTE: When calculating how many leaves of veneer I need for a particular project, I always order at least two extra sheets to be used just for repairs.

The Cloud Punch

Medium sized voids (0.5″ to 2″) can be repaired with a cloud punch tool. A cloud punch simply punches out an irregularly shaped hole and a matching plug is used to fill the hole. The irregular shape helps conceal the perimeter seam.

Place the cloud punch completely over the void, and firmly whack the punch once. I like to use a medium-soft substrate such as lightweight MDF (medium density fiberboard) or poplar hardwood for support. This is firm enough to allow the cut, but not so hard that it dulls the punch blade.

Remove damaged area.

Slide an extra sheet of veneer under the punched hole and locate an area that matches the surrounding grain. Mark a registration line to transfer to the punch for proper alignment.

Align the punch with the registration and tap it smartly to make the cut.

NOTE: This plug cut is a compression cut. No kerf is created and the seam will swell tight during taping and gluing.

Place the perfectly match plug into the damaged hole and veneer tape it (face side up) into place.

I like to create a repair that matches similar defects in the surrounding veneer. This method is much easier than trying to mimic the surrounding grain for an invisible repair. The patch on the left matches the natural knot on the right. The open crack will be filled during the finishing process.

For large repairs, a custom cloud punch can be made from a piece of electrical conduit (EMT). You can also make this repair with multiple punches using a smaller punch, but a single larger punch creates a cleaner repair.

TO MAKE A CUSTOM PUNCH, start with a 6″ long piece of EMT, .5″ larger than the repair. Use a Dremel™ tool, hand file or die grinder to sharpen the inside edge. It is important to put the bevel on the inside as this will compress the veneer patch while punching. If the bevel is on the outside edge, you will split the repair hole open while punching.

Shape the pipe to form an irregular cloud. Note: the more asymmetrical the shape, the less conspicuous the repair will be. The pipe can be stretched out to form a long narrow amoeba shape too. Make it any size to conform to the repair required.

Collect 'em, trade 'em with your fellow woodworkers.

You can hone the edge lightly with a sharpening stone as well as heat-treat the edge for a longer lasting and cleaner cut. In addition, the forming process can distort the flatness of the cutting edge: The punch can be re-flattened and the bevel refined with a file.

The punching and repair process is the same as using a commercial punch. The flattening process softens the veneer, making it much easier to cut, punch, and handle.

Double Bevel Cutting and Technique

The double bevel cutting technique incorporates a fine scroll saw and is the same cutting method used in many marquetry inlays.

The general idea is that you are cutting a patch that is shaped like a cork that has a beveled edge. As the patch is pushed into a hole it gets more and more snug. With this method, the hole also has a matching bevel edge so the fit is perfect and flush.

The cutting bevel angle should be roughly 14 degrees. This essentially creates a cork-shaped plug that fits perfectly into the hole. This angled cut line creates a scarf joint that helps easily conceal the seam. More on this on pp. 47-48.

Place a matching piece under the hole and align the grain as best as you can.

Draw out a general cutting path on the top piece of veneer. Anchor the two pieces of veneer together with masking tape to help hold the alignment in place while cutting. Here I use mineral spirits to help see the finished color.

I typically use my power scroll saw to perform this inlay. The cut can also be performed with a handheld scroll saw if it will reach. Alternatively, the cut can be performed freehand or by making a template out of 1/8″ hardboard and cutting by hand using an Exacto® knife.

Drill a small blade access hole on the inside of the cutting path line.

For scroll sawing, feed the saw blade through both layers of veneer.

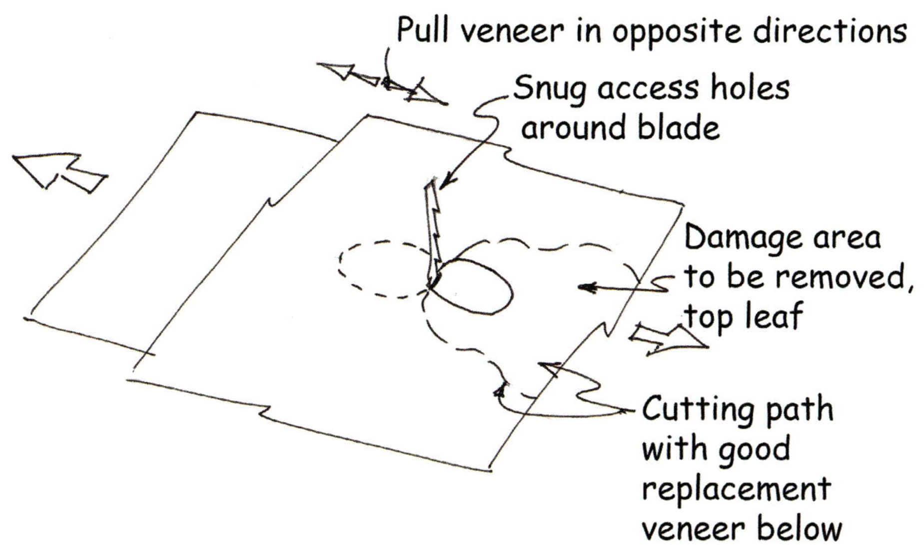

Release the anchor tape. Slightly move the veneer in opposite directions, pushing the top piece of veneer inward and the bottom outward, offsetting the two holes to fit snuggly on both sides of the blade. Do not rotate the alignment. Re-tape the two pieces of veneer together.

Set the blade or bed angle at 14 degrees and cut the patch out following the drawn path. This is a double bevel cut.

The cutting angle varies depending on the thickness of the veneer and blade. If the veneer is thicker the angle decreases. Typically 12-14 degrees should do the trick for a 1/42 thick veneer and a 2/0 blade (see page 55 for more on blades).

WHICH DIRECTION TO CUT?

This can get a bit confusing, and it is important that your patch (the piece that is being installed) is beveled in the correct direction so it matches the hole.

QUESTIONS TO ASK YOURSELF ARE:

- Are you cutting the patch from the top or the bottom ?
- Are you installing your patch from the top or bottom?
- Which way is your blade angled?
- Are you cutting clockwise or counter clockwise?

Confused yet? Hang in there.

Visualize making a cork and make a test cut first. Cut a circle and if it is too small, then cut in the other direction.

Here is another way to describe and visualize this cut: If you're replacing from the bottom, the bottom-most faces will have the widest dimension. See the top illustration.

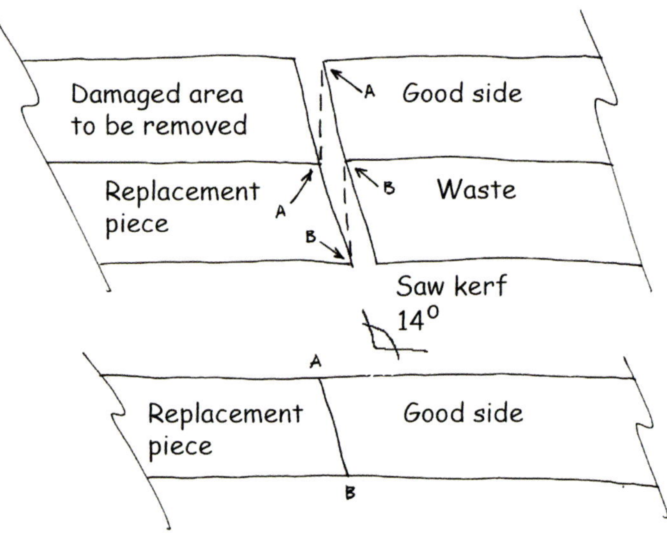

The angle compensates for the blade kerf and aligns the two good pieces of veneer to match perfectly.

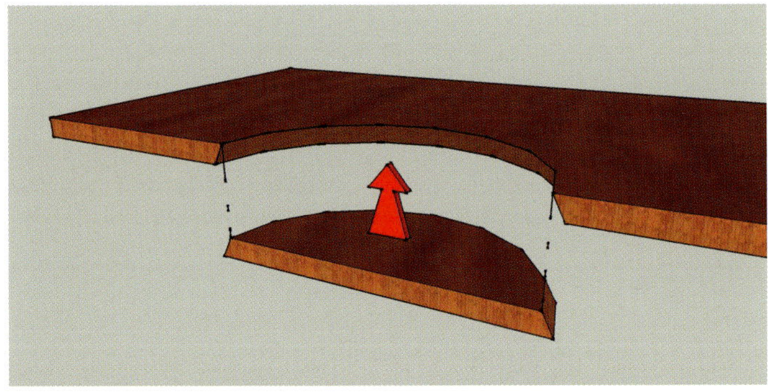

The replacement piece as shown from the bottom. Notice the angle of the bevel. This hole can be cut in either direction (clockwise or counterclockwise) depending if the blade (bevel) is angled left or right.

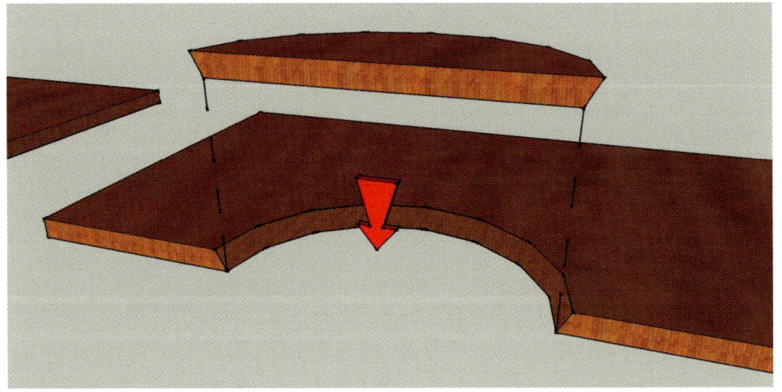

Installed patch from the top.

The tapered plug self aligns and fits as snug as a bug in a rug.

THE THREE PLUG REPAIRS, FROM LEFT TO RIGHT:
Commercial cloud punch, homemade punch, and hand (scroll saw) cut.

This double bevel cutting technique can be used to extend your veneer by filling in large missing corners or replacing unwanted figures in the grain.

This olive ash burl has a missing corner and a large unwanted light area.

Find a similar area in your extra piece of veneer.

Tape a piece of tracing paper over the veneer to be repaired.

Trace the perimeter of the full piece you want and define some general grain patterns near the area you wish to replace.

Put the replacement veneer under the tracing paper and align with the traced grain.

Tape the replacement piece to the good veneer below.

Using a piece of carbon paper (white versions are available for use with darker woods), trace a cutting seam line onto the repair veneer leaf. Follow the grain pattern as best as possible. The "squigglier" the line, the better the repair will blend in.

The transferred line can be faint and may need to be darkened.

In this example, the olive ash was not flattened, so I taped over the seam to be cut. This helps prevent chipping during the cut. White veneer tape allows you to see through to the cutting line. For more on tape, see Chapter 8, Taping, page 100.

Cut through both layers of veneer at a 14-degree angle, following the predetermined seam. Since this cut is not circular (creating a cork as in the last repair) the cutting direction or blade angle is not an issue.

The two halves match perfectly. Tape the two halves together. It is okay to tape over tape.

SCROLL SAW BLADES – There is a wide variety of blade sizes and tooth configurations (see drawing) available on the market. Blade sizes range from 7 TPI (teeth per inch) to 5/0 (56 TPI). A simple internet search reveals more styles and marketing ploys to confuse even the most experienced woodworker. To keep it simple, I like to use a double skip tooth, 2/0 blade. This will give you a nice clean cut and minimal kerf.

1 2 3 4 5 6 7 8

BLADE TYPES FROM LEFT TO RIGHT:
1. standard, 2. single skip tooth, 3. double skip tooth, 4. reverse tooth, 5. top cut, 6. crown, 7. spiral, 8. flat spiral

The original leaf on the left and new patched leaf on the right.

Other Repair Methods After The Veneer Is Pressed To The Core

Repairing Bubbles

Occasionally veneer bubbles may appear due to too much glue, not enough glue, veneer stress (flattening helps relieve this), or early removal from the press. Many times these can be ironed back down, however, this will only work if you are using a PVA (polyvinyl acetate) glue. More on glue in Chapter 10.

Be sure not to overheat the iron as this can burn the wood and/or release glue in the surrounding areas.

It is important that all the veneer is completely glued down before sanding or finishing. If not, this will only wreak havoc down the road: loose veneer eventually shows up.

Simply set a household iron on a medium heat (synthetic) setting *without steam* and firmly press the bubble down 15-30 seconds or so. The heat will reactivate the PVA glue and hold the veneer in place. You can remove the heat and continue pressing with a hard block of wood or a veneer roller until the glue is cool.

Stubborn bubbles need to be cut open and re-glued. By lightly tapping the surface with the tip of your finger, you can hear a lighter-pitched sound where it is loose. Carefully find and mark the perimeter of the loose veneer, and cut the bubble open at a low angle. Try to follow a natural grain line.

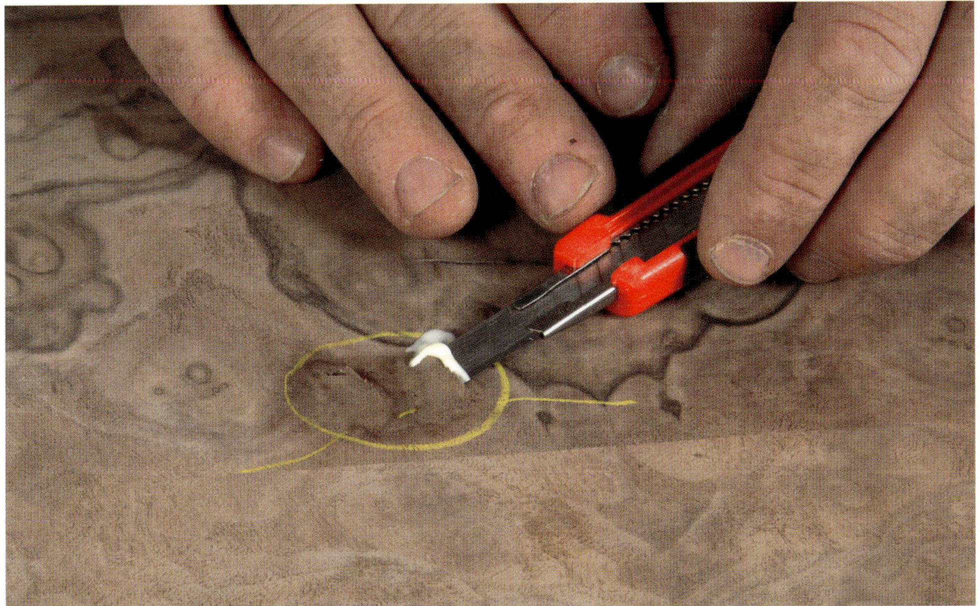

Inject some glue with either a syringe or the end of a small utility knife. Press it down and squish the glue all around under the veneer to be sure it gets everywhere.

Iron the bubble down, clamp or place a small heavy weight on the area until the glue sets.

Repairing Larger Cracks and Voids

Larger cracks and voids need to be repaired with a filler. Sawdust and PVA or "super" glue (CA or cyanoacrylate glue) works well for home putty formulations.

I often use an acetone-based filler such as Famowood™. This putty dries fast, doesn't shrink, fills easily, accepts stain, and the different tones are intermixable for color matching.

You can use a manufacturer's solvent or straight acetone to thin it out. The solvent will reconstitute older dry putty and I like to add a splash to my putty can before I close the lid and put it back in on the shelf.

Tape around the void to protect the surrounding grain while applying the putty.

NOTE: It's important to tape around the repair to avoid filling in the surrounding grain with putty.

Simply press the putty into the void with a small putty knife or painter's spatula. The tape will leave the filler slightly above the veneer surface for future sanding.

Remove the tape after the putty is dry and sand it flush.

For larger cracks, I prefer to use lighter filler for color touch-up during the finishing process. If I am filling a small knot hole, I use a darker color to emulate surrounding, existing knots.

Sanding

An entire book could be dedicated to sanding, so I will give you my simple version.

Sanding veneer can sound scary: Is it so thin that I will sand through with one stroke? Certainly, one should be careful, but typically sand-through happens when using an improper sanding technique. Of course, this has to do with the species of wood and thickness, for example, softer veneers such as redwood burl will sand faster than walnut burl.

The final desired finish needs to be determined before setting the sanding schedule. For example, if a closed pore, hand rubbed, high-gloss sheen finish is called for, then the veneer surface needs to be perfectly flat. This sounds obvious, but smaller sanders can easily leave subtle low spots that can show up after the final finish is applied.

On the other hand, if you want an open pore, off the gun, satin sheen for the final finish, then the surface doesn't need to be perfectly flat. In addition, darker woods show sanding imperfections more than lighter woods.

Various sanders; from left to right; 6″ electric, 5″ pneumatic, 9″ pneumatic, 35 lb in-line Stir™ (pneumatic)

My general sand schedule is as follows:

- Flatten the entire surface with straight line sander, 9″ orbital sander, or by hand, using a large, flat sanding block, using 120 grit (depending on final finish).
- Lightly wipe the entire surface down with a moist sponge to raise the grain. Note: This will also reveal any remaining glue glaze (see page 108) and loose veneer that form bubbles. Better that you find them now instead of your client finding them down the road.
- Use a 5″ or 6″ inch random orbital sander (mine is pneumatic) with a medium 3/16″ stroke. Straight AND orbital sanders come with different

I use my 9″ orbital sander or a straight line, 35-pound Stir™ that is designed to flatten a surface. Sanding by hand with a large flat sanding block will work too, but you need a lot more elbow grease.

stroke sizes, 3/8″, 3/16″ and 3/32″. I use 3/8″ and 3/16″ for raw wood; 3/32″ for finish sanding. I use the larger for sanding raw wood and the smaller for sanding finishes.

- Sand the entire surface using even pressure, taking slow, full strokes that overlap the previous pass by half the sanding pad. Do the entire surface three or four times, changing the sanding path direction by 45 or 90 degrees after each sanding of the entire surface. Do not sand quickly back and forth like you are hand sanding, this will leave large swirl marks. Let the sander do the work.
- Start with 120 grit sandpaper, then 180, then 220. The sequence of grits will depend on the density (hardness) of the wood.

On some occasions, I lightly hit the surface with 80 grit paper for veneer tape removal or unusually high spots. If you are trying to make a living at this, I suggest doing a variety of samples with various sequences of paper first.

(I had one employee who insisted on using what seemed to be every grit known to mankind: 80,100, 120, 150, 180, 220, 320. In lieu of firing the stubborn son-of-a-gun, I simply sanded the same species with only two grits, 120 and 180, and finished both samples in the same manner. He couldn't tell the difference, and I saved a lot of time and money.)

One controversial saying is, "there is nothing better than good enough." The point is: don't over sand. This is one way of avoiding a sand-though. This is another reason to lay up a test sample.

SOME SANDING TIPS:

- Do a test sanding and finish with the proper sheen as the final finish will be.
- Do a test sand-through on your test panel.
- Sand evenly, do not focus on one area to remove a defect.
- DON'T use the edge of your sander, keep the sander flat at all times.
- To go after a specific defect, sand by hand or use a scraper for more control.
- On edges, only overhang the sander by a 1/4 of the sanding pad.
- After the final sanding, wipe the entire surface with mineral spirits to help reveal any remaining defects.
- Remove the sanding dust between each paper change as the dust may contain a larger grit from the previous paper grade and may continue to scratch the surface.
- Take your time and sand thoroughly, three passes minimum for each grit.

NOTE: I will say this only once.

NEVER EVER use a handheld belt sander on veneer.
Never, never, never.

Repairs Made After Finishing

Most projects require some sort of touch up during the finishing process, so it's a good idea to practice, practice, practice on sample boards before a critical repair rears its ugly head.

Many products are available for touch up repairs and worthy of another whole book.

After sanding, spray a light coat of gloss finish over the entire surface. I like to use lacquer. This helps reveal the true color of the wood and lets me "see" any surface defects such as sanding swirls, tape shadows, slicing score lines and/or natural defects.

If there are any sanding defects present, re-sand the area and lightly finished again. Use a gloss sheen finish, as the flattening agents in a satin or dull finish will build up and leave a witness line (a light haze where the different layers of flattening agents build up and change the sheen).

This photo shows my standard set of repair supplies, from top center, clockwise:

- Aerosol lacquer for quick spot finishing and color testing.
- Shellac: I like to use an aerosol as it has a longer shelf life.
- Alcohol: For my shellac and pigment color work
- Famowood™ solvent or acetone.
- Famowood™ putty.
- Wax putty sticks and putty knife.
- Color markers.
- Blendal® powder stains (aniline powders) and #4 brush.

Once any scratches and the like are removed, go after small knot holes with wax filler sticks. Use a darker color than the surrounding veneer, typically dark brown or black. These holes will read as obvious knots. Filling them with lighter putty can make them look like they have been "filled." Notice the longer crack that was filled with lighter filler (p.58-59), and now requires color work.

Coloring Repairs

For repairs that require more fine tuning, color and grain can be painted in using an aniline powder pigment / shellac mix.

Observation is key to color matching. Many veneers, especially burls, can be a complex combination of subtle color layers and grain directions.

It is often easier to start with a lighter color first and apply darker layers afterwards. Experience is the key, so practice, practice, practice.

Below is my approach to color matching and application of color layers.

In brief, a base color is matched and painted down on the veneer repair, typically the lightest color in the wood. Once a base color is applied it is sealed in with finish (I use gloss lacquer).

Next, apply a different color that matches the second lightest color over the first layer.

This application technique seals in each layer and allows you to erase unacceptable layers of color as you work. For example, after sealing the first layer of color, if the second layer of color is not acceptable it can be erased (more on this below.) Once the second color is applied, it is also sealed in. This step is repeated until all the subtle layers are achieved.

For simple knots, typically one color will do. For multi-color repairs, two or three layers of color are common.

To mix aniline powders I use a non-waxed paper cup as a mixing pallet and a #4 brush. The #4 brush size allows you to produce a fine tip and will hold enough pigment to cover a generous repair area. Often I see students with the finest brush they could buy and cutting off all but three hairs. This type of brush has its place but will not hold enough pigment for general repairs.

THE MIXING IS SIMPLE: pour a small amount of shellac into a non-waxed paper cup. I like to add a drop or so of alcohol to thin the mixture. Older shellac can get gummy and if past its shelf life will not dry. I always use fresh shellac.

Dip the brush into the shellac and then dip into the aniline powdered pigment, choosing a color close to the repair. (It is rare that the pigment will exactly match the veneer.) Use the side of the cup as a pallet to collect the pigmented shellac. Then gather another color in the same manner picking another "close" color.

A good eye for color and some understanding of basic color theory is helpful.

Gather up two or three colors and apply them around the top edge of the non-wax paper cup. Blend them together to create just the right color

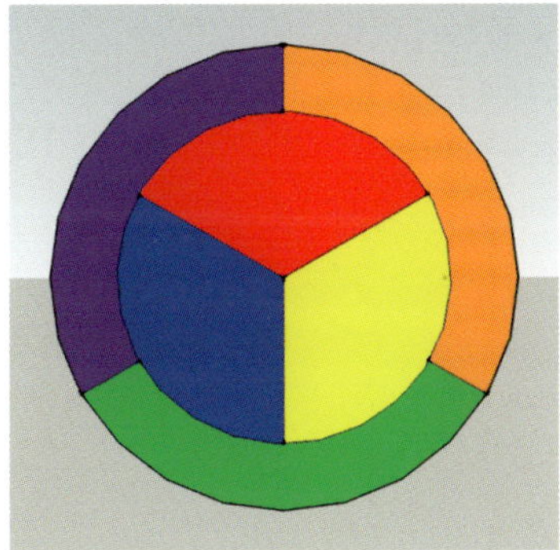

Color wheel showing primary colors Red, Yellow, and Blue from which all other colors can be created. The outer ring shows secondary colors Orange, Green, and Purple.

Primary colors are red, yellow and blue, and with white and black, all other colors can be made (I am not suggesting you use only these five colors.)

Mixing: see color wheel.

- Red and yellow make orange
- Yellow and blue make green
- Blue and red make purple

Adding the opposite color on the color wheel neutralizes or "greys" the color.

For example, if you have a reddish brown and want more orange, add a touch of yellow. Then you might lighten it up with some white and add some blue to reduce the pastel look and grey it up.

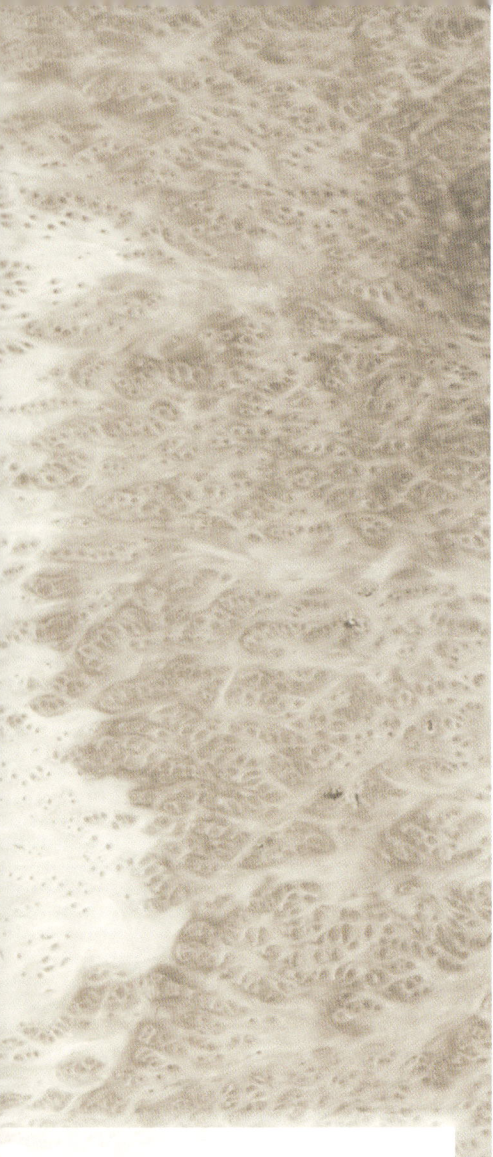

Typically, I gather up two or three colors first and apply them around the top edge of the cup. I blend them together to form a number of intermixed puddles between, going back and forth to subtly adjust the color.

When you think you have a close match, test the color pigment first on the veneer close to the repair. If it doesn't match, simply wipe with alcohol to erase the spot.

This is the reason I put a light coat of lacquer finish on the veneer, to show the true veneer color, as well as protect the raw veneer from absorbing any touch up pigments. This is the basis of the touch-up method: the alcohol doesn't affect a lacquer finish and it allows the touch up material to be erased.

There are many techniques and variations to this method that could easily take another book in itself. Don't be afraid to play and experiment. If you're not happy, simply erase with alcohol and try again. When you get really good you can skip the layers and erasing option.

Testing on a piece of glass or clear Mylar™ (plastic) over the veneer is another way to test the matched color without having to use alcohol to erase. It also works if you are using stains to touch up, or if you are attempting to repair unfinished wood or a shellac-finished piece.

For a few reasons, use the least possible amount of pigment. First, too much pigment will actually build up into a mound on the veneer surface. This will possibly get sanded off during the clear coat finishing and sanding process and/or it can show up as a bump. Second, a transparent layer of color will often be more visually convincing. It is not always necessary for your mixture to be a solid opaque color.

NOTE: All wood changes color over time and the color repair won't, so creating a fake knot or imperfection eliminates this issue. For example; if you've matched a cherry repair perfectly, when the real cherry wood darkens over time the repair will not. It will appear lighter and become an obvious repair.

SOME TECHNIQUES TO TRY:

- Don't paint in just the damaged area, but continue to paint grain lines past the repair. This draws attention away from the repair.
- Look for other imperfections, such as mineral stains, knots, and the like, and mimic them with the pigment. Try not to perfectly match a repair to its surroundings, but turn it into a defect or knot. I have even been known to create other defects throughout the piece to convince (my client) that they are ALL natural. For example, on a clean piece of maple with no defects, adding one or two other small mineral stains in addition to your repair adds continuity (just don't tell anyone!).
- Another technique to try is similar to watercolor painting, where you apply a thin coat of alcohol to the veneer first, then apply the pigmented shellac to an edge of the alcohol puddle. The pigment will bleed across the puddle in a gradation of color. This visual effect is often found in burl veneers. Again, observation and practice is the key to matching swirling colors in burl.
- To add grain texture, wait until the shellac is dry, then cut grain indentations through the repaired surface with a utility knife.
- Special markers and some colored pencils can also be used to paint in fine grain lines.
- One of my favorite tools is my finger, used for smudging, blending, and blurring.

If you're feeling confident, you can mix pigments into the final finish, such as lacquer and varnish, or if you must, polyurethane. The only drawback is that you can not erase any mistakes.

Lastly, in lieu of using aniline pigments, micro-tint or liquid aniline dyes can be used. They contain no pigment, absorb in raw wood easily and are transparent. They can also be added to shellac or to the final finish and applied in a similar manner.

Dyes are good for slight color spectrum shifting and applying directly on a finish. (Keep in mind that this is risky and not reversible.) Since dyes are transparent, it is more difficult and impossible in some cases to hide or completely change a color as with a pigmented "paint" application.

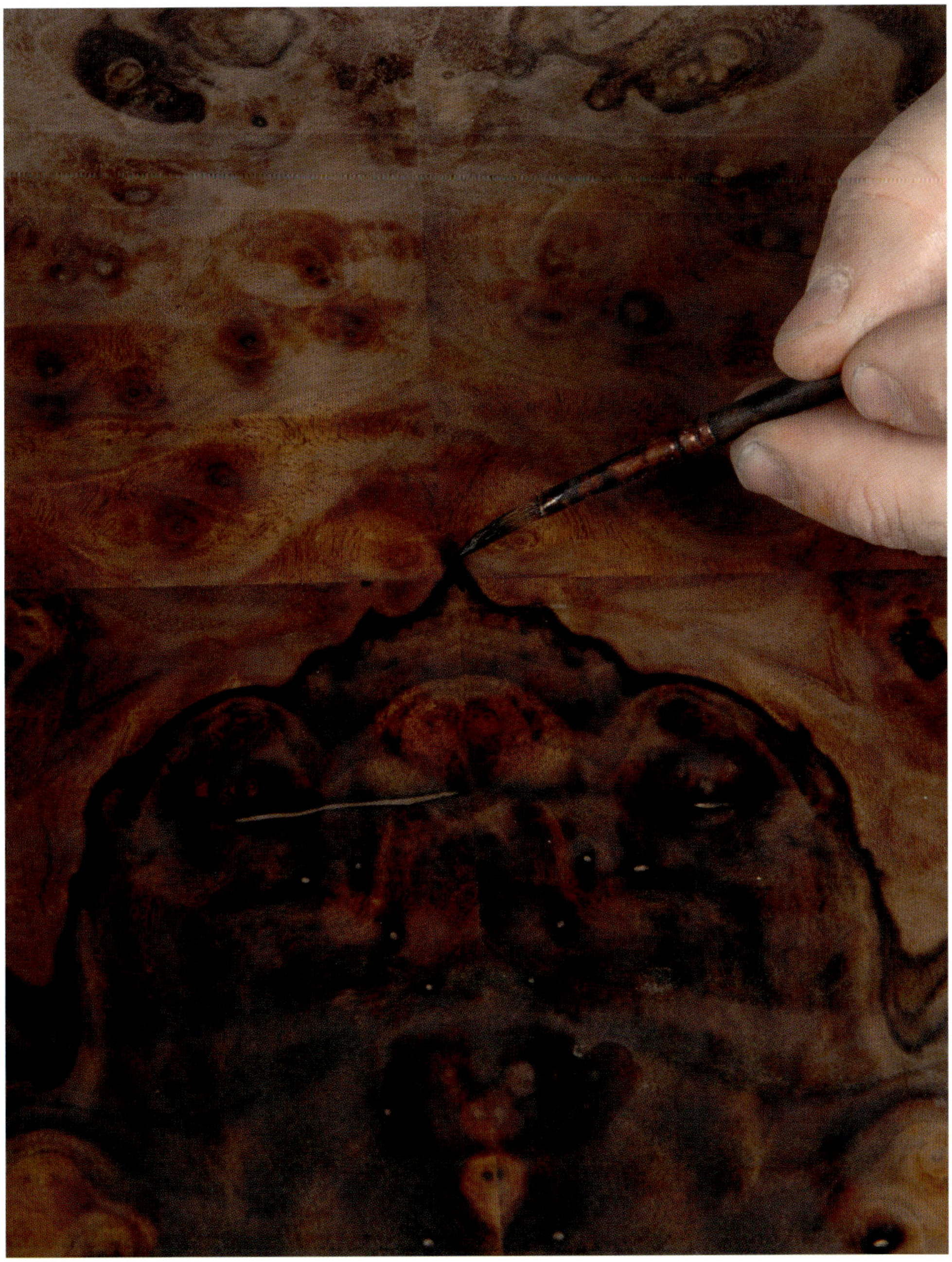

Use alcohol to bleed pigment. Here I demonstrate this technique on a piece of white plastic laminate to emphasis the effect. Wiping with a paper towel can add a hard edge to one side of the spill. See top right of puddle.

A simple repair extending the grain across the straight seam in a slip match .

5
Layout Examples

In this chapter you'll see various layouts created from a single leaf of redwood burl with contrasting sapwood. In following chapters, I demonstrate how to layout and seam the veneer to create these different patterns.

Determining the layout is the visual "art" of working with veneer.

Traditionally, when working with burls, symmetrical patterns are created using a book match system. A book match is when two veneer leaves are opened up like pages in a book. The grain pattern is mirrored along the joining edge, creating a symmetrical image.

Book matching can be arranged in a variety of configurations including two leaf, four square, checkerboard, diamond patterns, and radial (a circle or sunburst made up of pie-shaped wedges).

This is how it has been done for centuries: most designs were based on the book match system and all produced symmetrical patterns. That is, until now.

There are many ways to create asymmetrical patterns using methods such as slip, spin or spiral match. All these matches can be enhanced when working with dominant grain or contrasting color changes within the single leaf of veneer.

The most dramatic layout, and my personal favorite, has a contrasting sapwood and heartwood within the veneer to create a pattern.

NOTE: Veneers with sapwood are becoming more difficult to find as many veneer manufacturers consider sapwood a defect and trim it off the veneer.

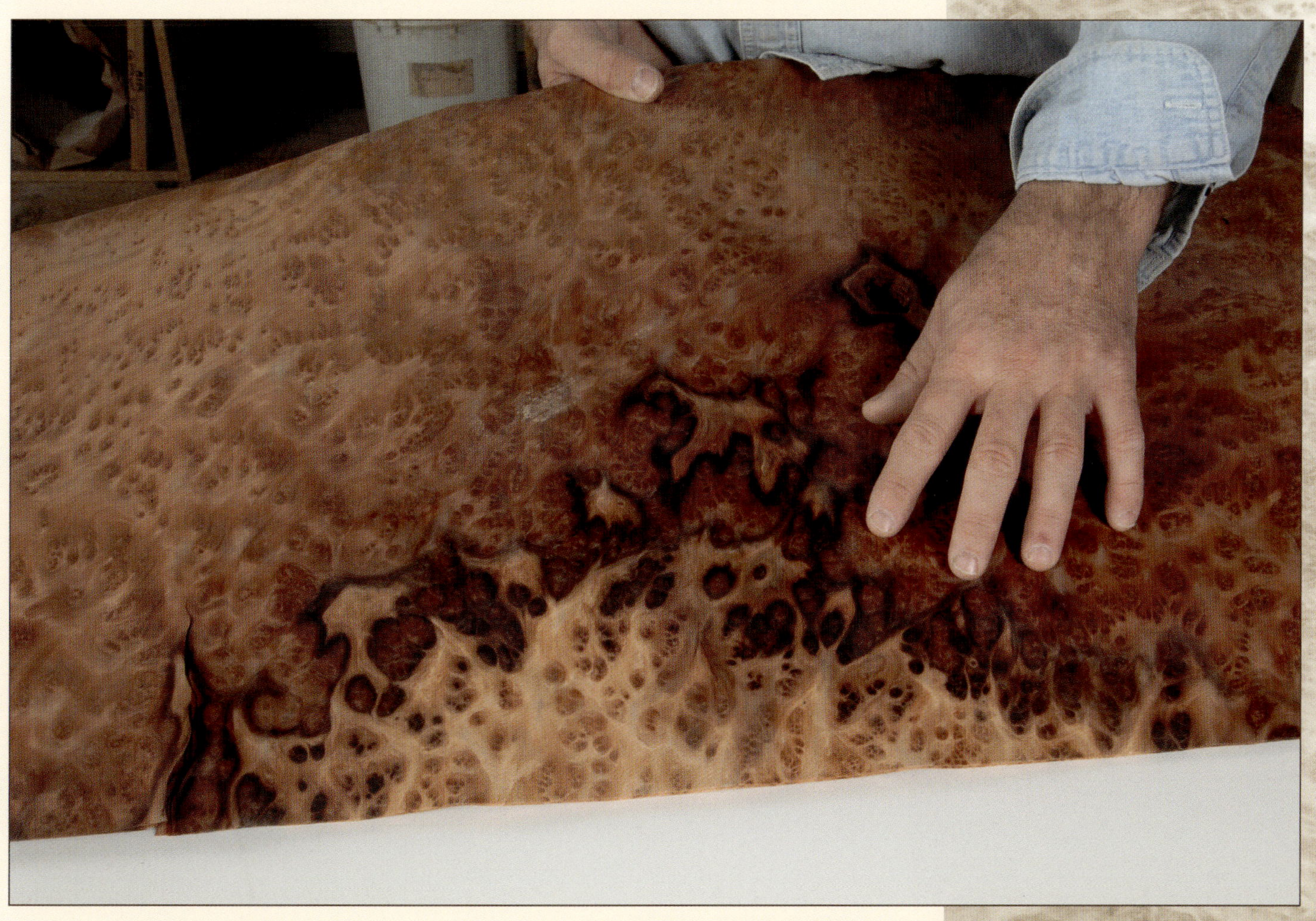

A choice example of sapwood in a redwood burl veneer. This specific sapwood figure is also referred to as "flame." Wow!

The following are visual examples of fundamental veneer matches. Understanding these types of matches expands your options and provides more creative freedom and control.

The following matches are performed with a straight seam and I find this very distracting. In Chapter 9, I demonstrate how this obvious straight seam can be disguised using my wavy contour seam.

With the use of a wavy contour seam the seam can be hidden, creating a naturally asymmetrical pattern. Traditionally burls are not slip matched as the pattern shows an obvious seam, especially with contrasting sap / heartwood areas as shown below. Slip matching is often done with straight grain veneers. Later you'll see how this can be effectively used with burls.

I will explain in Chapter 6 how to layout and sequence these leaves.

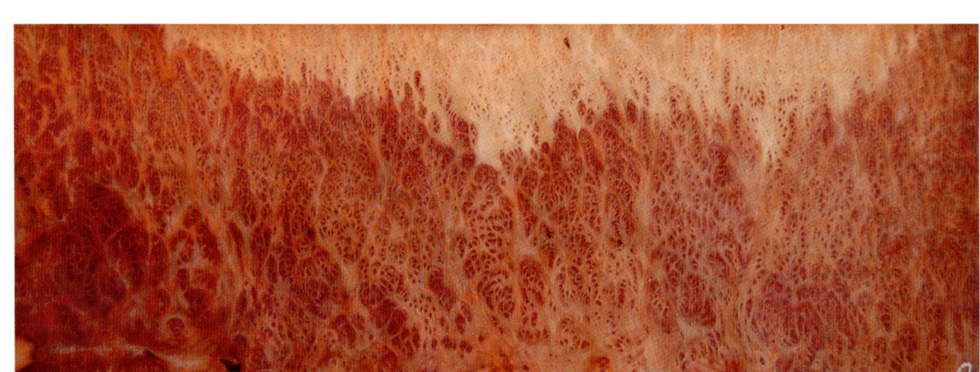

A single leaf of redwood burl with sapwood.

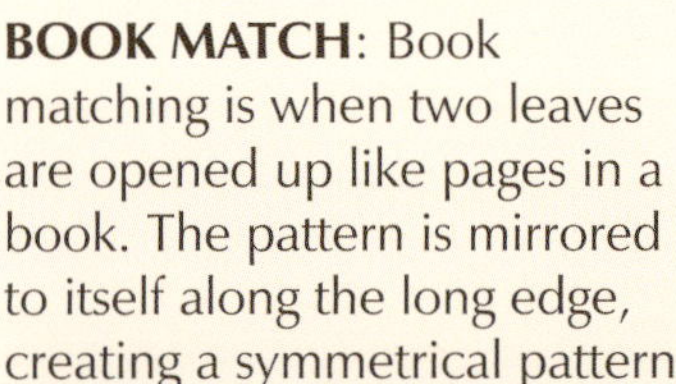

BOOK MATCH: Book matching is when two leaves are opened up like pages in a book. The pattern is mirrored to itself along the long edge, creating a symmetrical pattern.

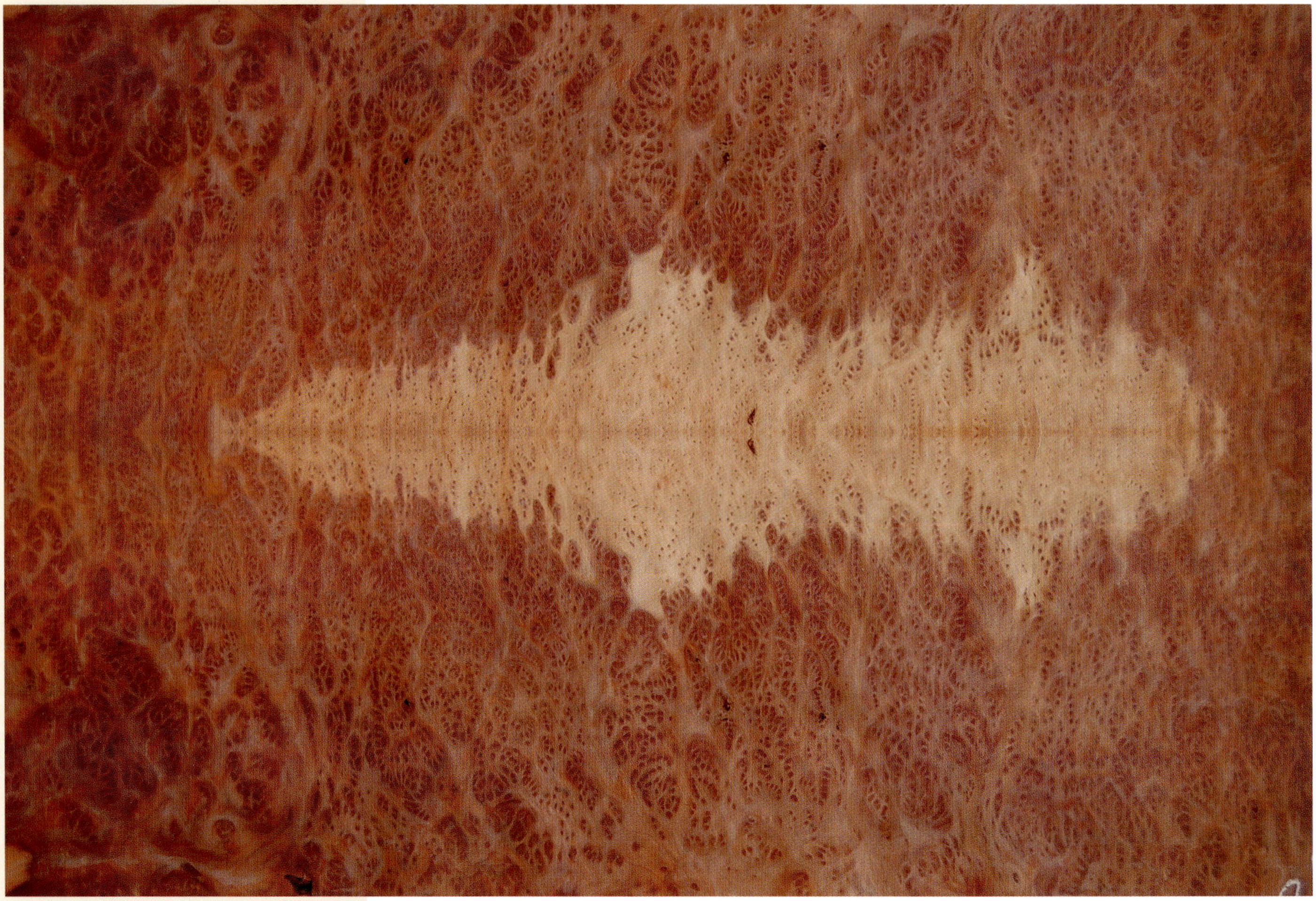

BOOK AND END (BOOK) MATCH: Four leaves matched, also referred to as a four square.

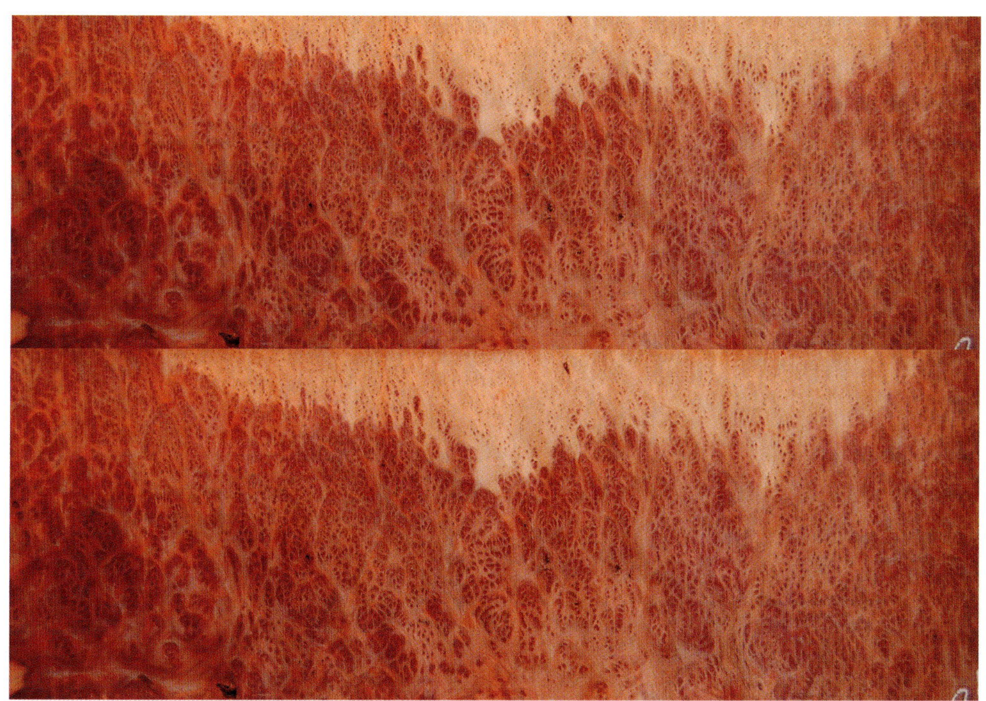

SLIP MATCH: This is when the leaves are not turned over, they are simply slid over each other and the opposite edges are seamed. The sapwood makes this obvious and typically this would never be done with burls and sapwood.

END SLIP MATCH OF TWO LEAVES: Note that the ends of each piece have been trimmed so the sapwood lines up. Depending on how consistent the grain and color is throughout the leaf, a slip match can add an asymmetrical pattern option to the design in lieu of the mirrored symmetrical patterns that book matching provides. More on how to align the sapwood in Chapter 11.

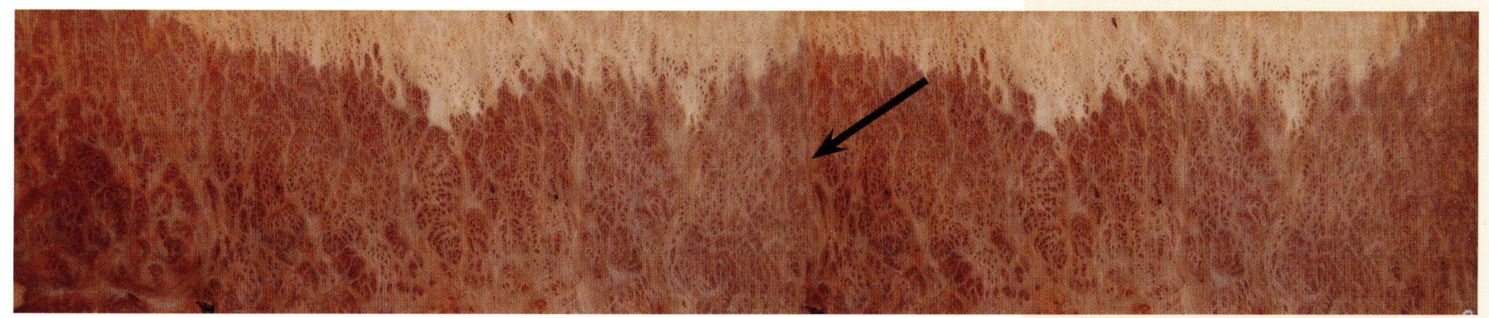

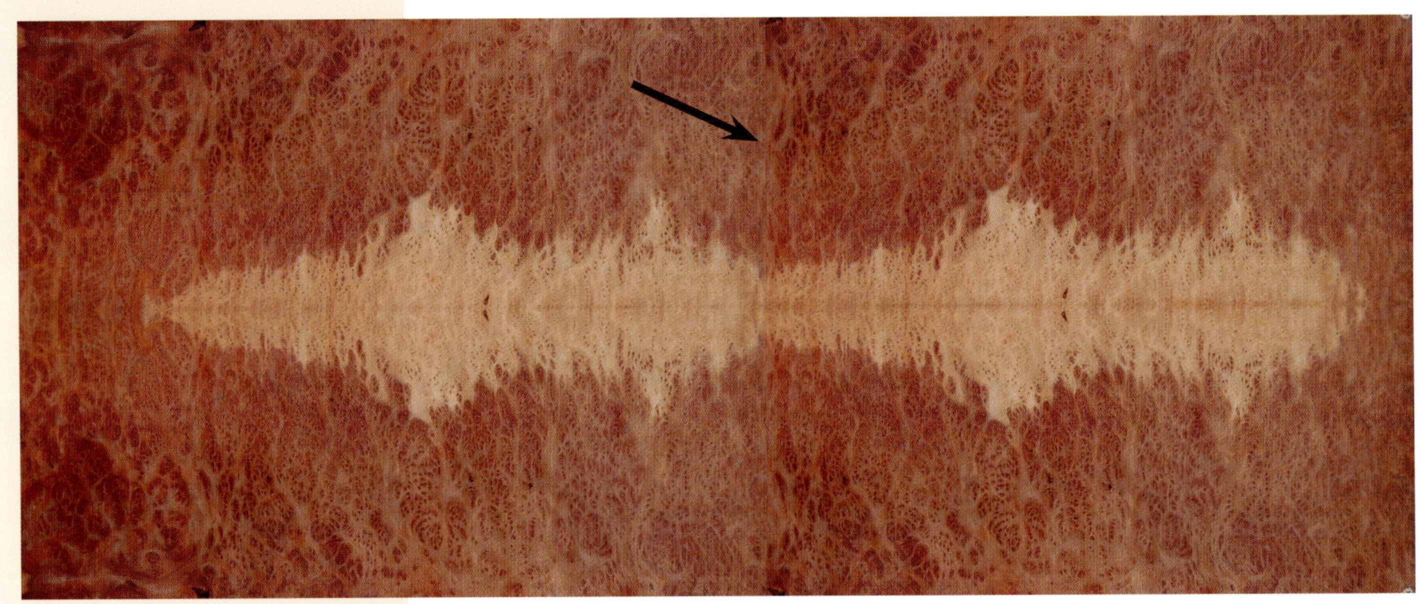

BOOK AND END SLIP MATCH OF FOUR LEAVES: book matched long edge, slip matched short ends. Again the ends are trimmed so the sapwood lines up. When repeated with more leaves, a nice pattern is created, although it is still symmetrical.

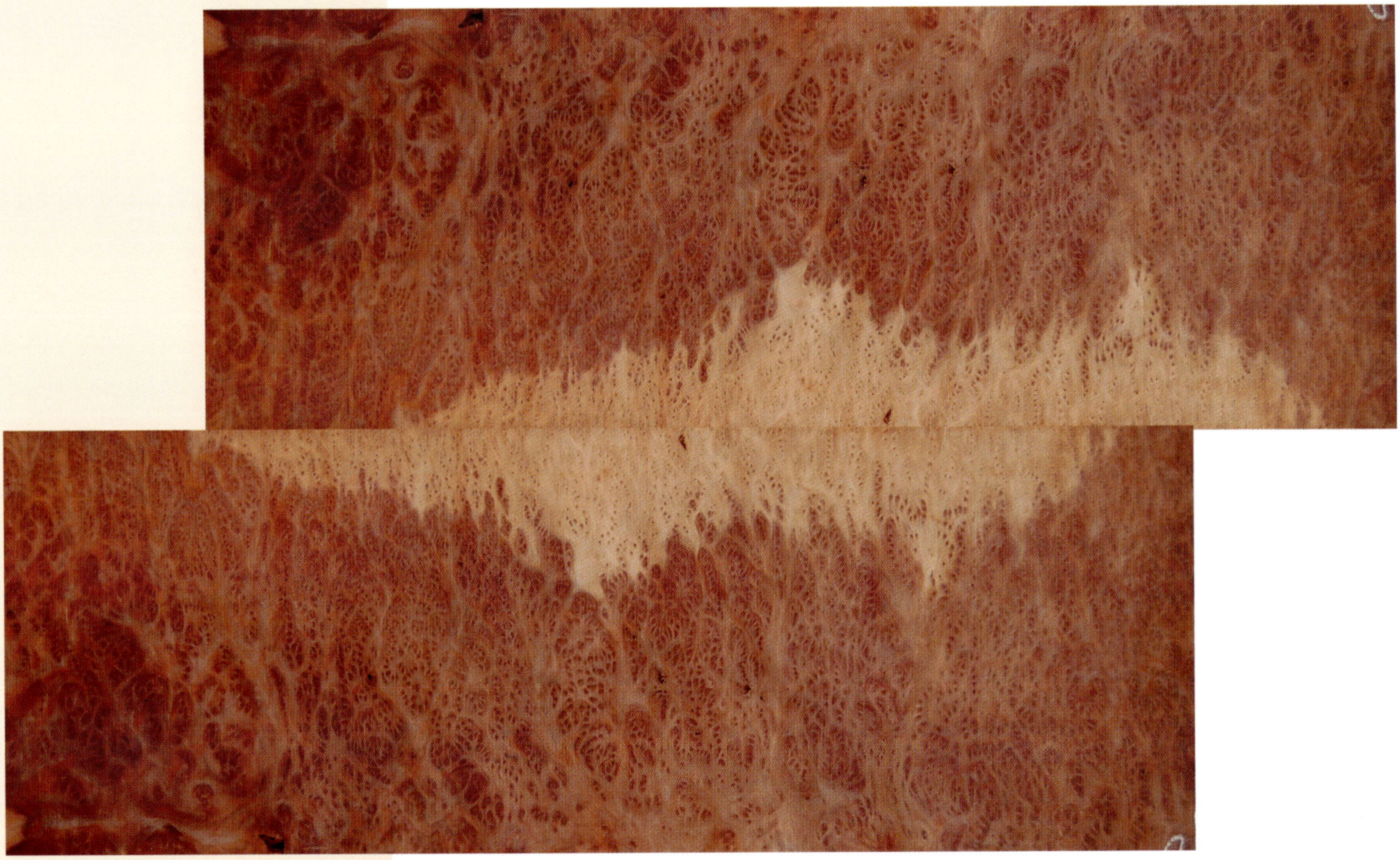

OFFSET BOOK MATCH: By simply offsetting a book match, an asymmetrical pattern can be generated. Now we're getting creative!

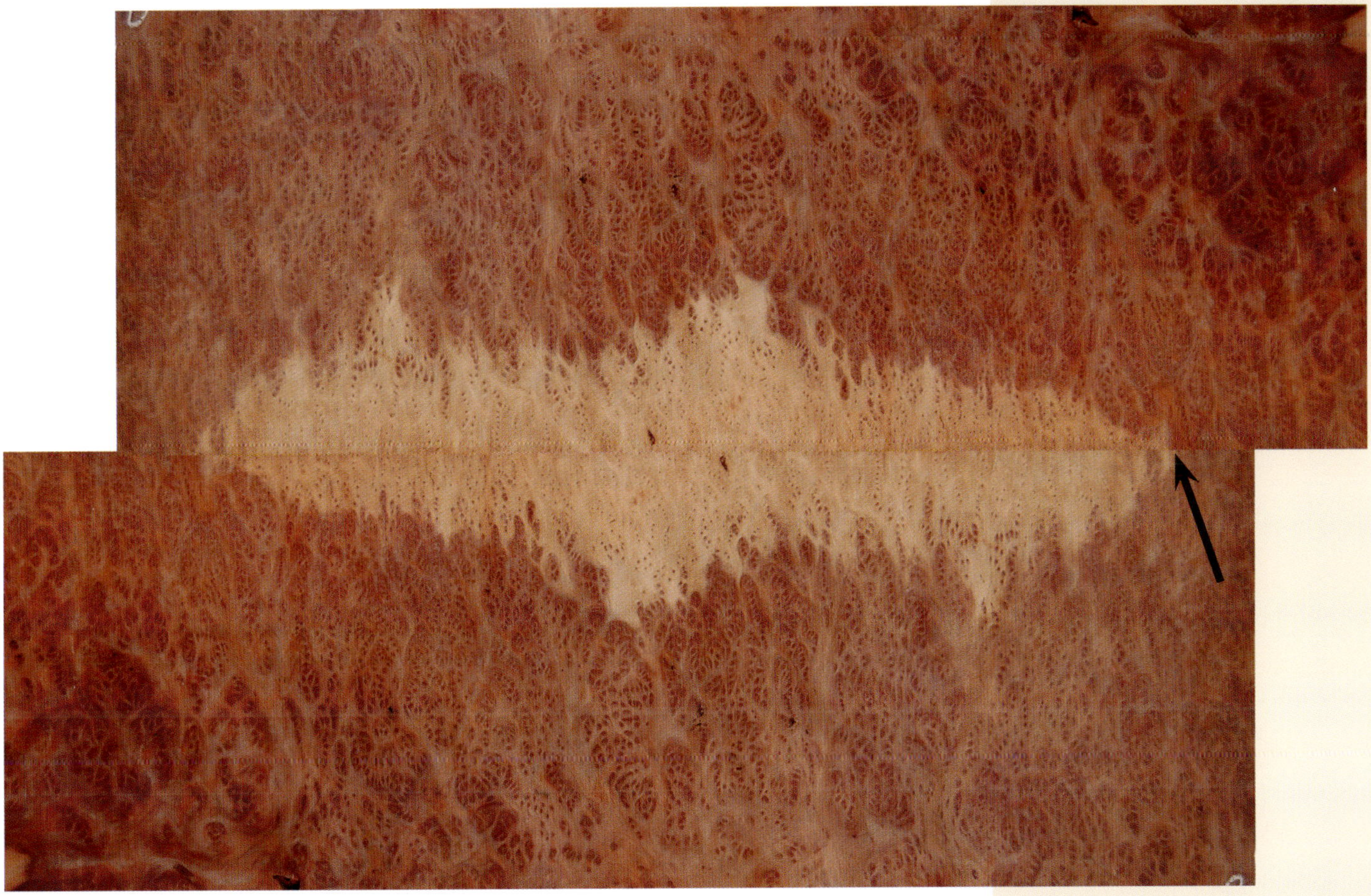

SPIN MATCH OF TWO LEAVES: One leaf is rotated 180 degrees and not turned over. The sapwood is aligned by shifting the leaves left to right. This match is a simple asymmetrical pattern. See pages 85-86.

OFFSET SPIN MATCH: Offsetting a spin match also creates an asymmetrical pattern, and can create a strange sort of reverse book match in the center.

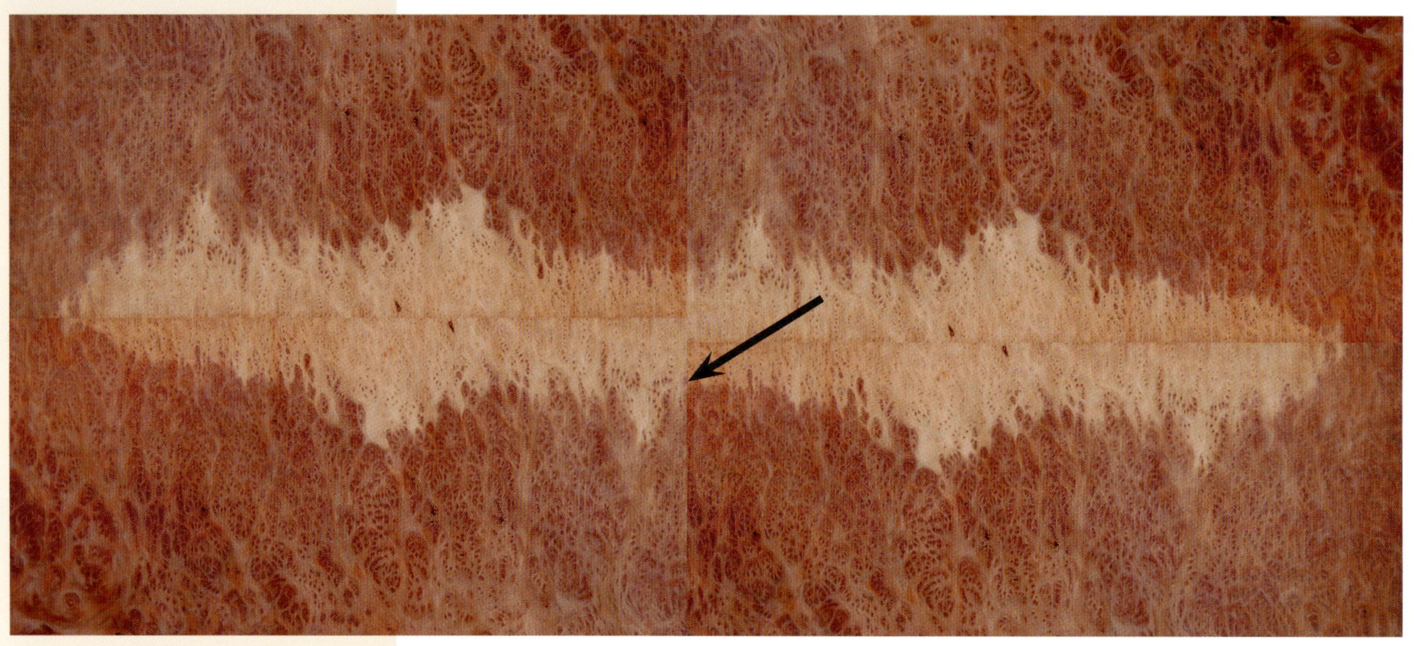

SPIN SLIP OF FOUR LEAVES: The end seam has been offset to align the sapwood.

SPIN BOOK: Spin the long edge, book match the ends. Here the top and bottom are asymmetrical and the left to right are mirrored, symmetrically.

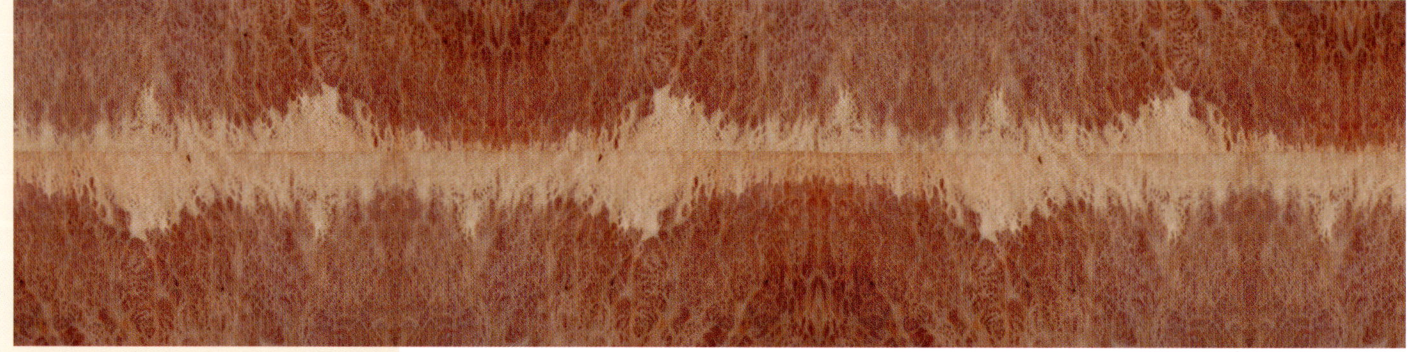

EIGHT PIECES: Book matched ends and spin match long edges. Here you can see how you can create a sapwood line that can vary in width.

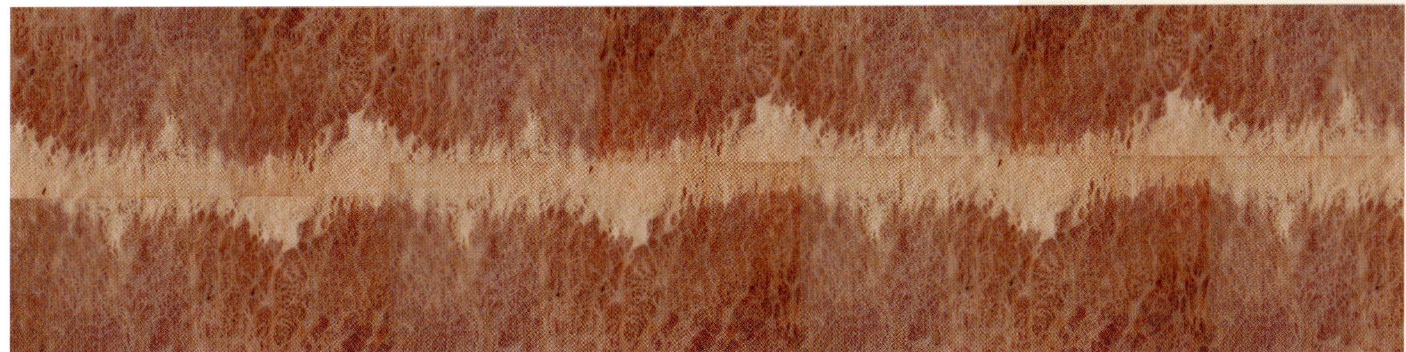

EIGHT PIECES: Book matched ends and slipped matched long edges. (thump thump...thump thump)

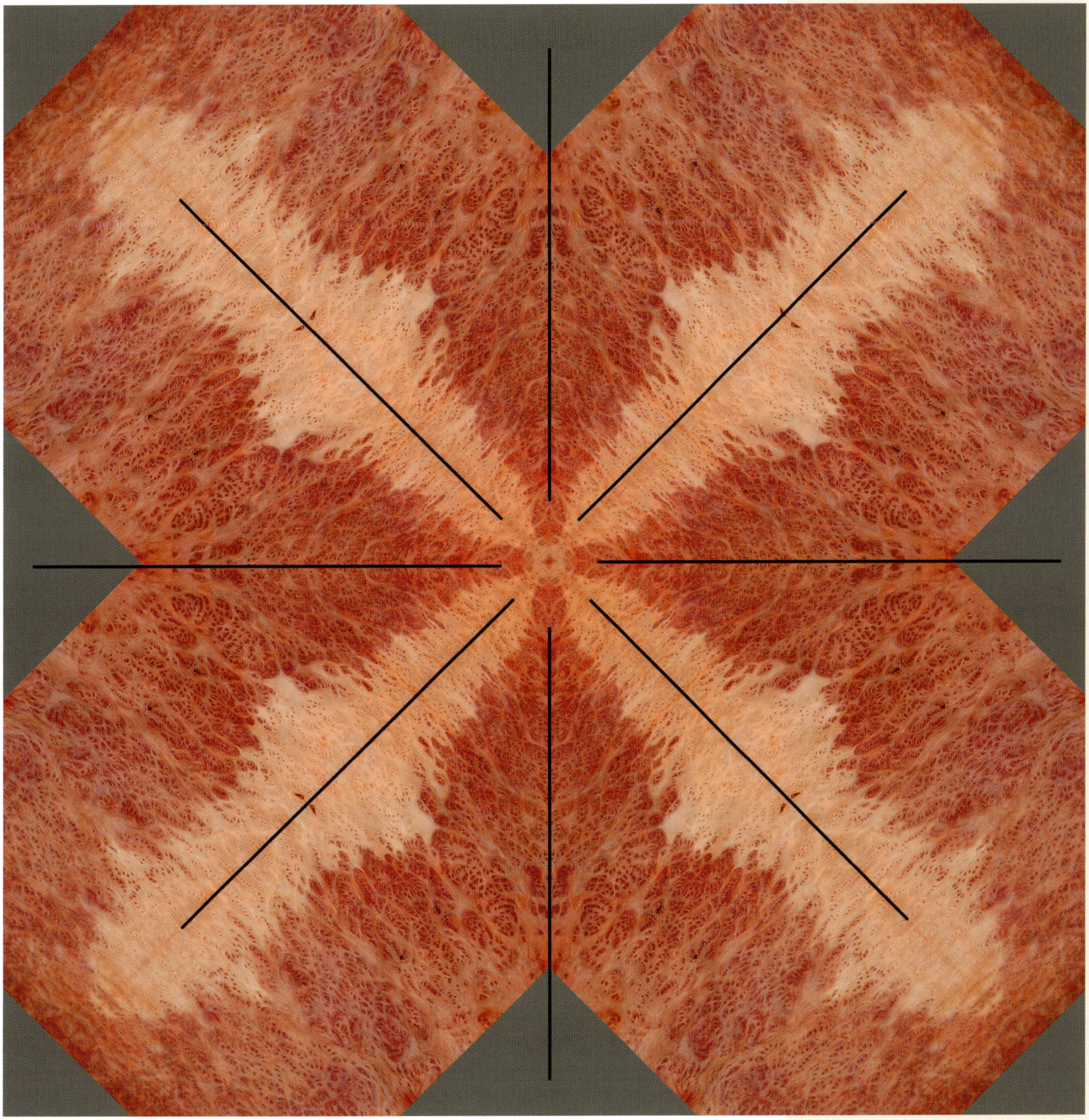

EIGHT-PIECE RADIAL: Four sets of book matched leaves are mitered together at 45 degrees joined in the center. See page 83 for more on this type of match.

The radial after trimming square. I find the straight seams extremely distracting. See Chapter 9, Wavy Contour Seam, for a new way to hide the straight seams.

REVERSE DIAMOND: Here four sets of book matched leaves are mitered together at 45 degrees, perpendicular to the book match seam. I've left the outside leaves untrimmed and included drawn-in lines to help visualize the layout.

REVERSE DIAMOND CROPPED

16-LEAF RADIAL MATCH: eight sets of book match.
See page 83 for layout methods.

CROPPED 16-LEAF RADIAL MATCH: eight sets of book match

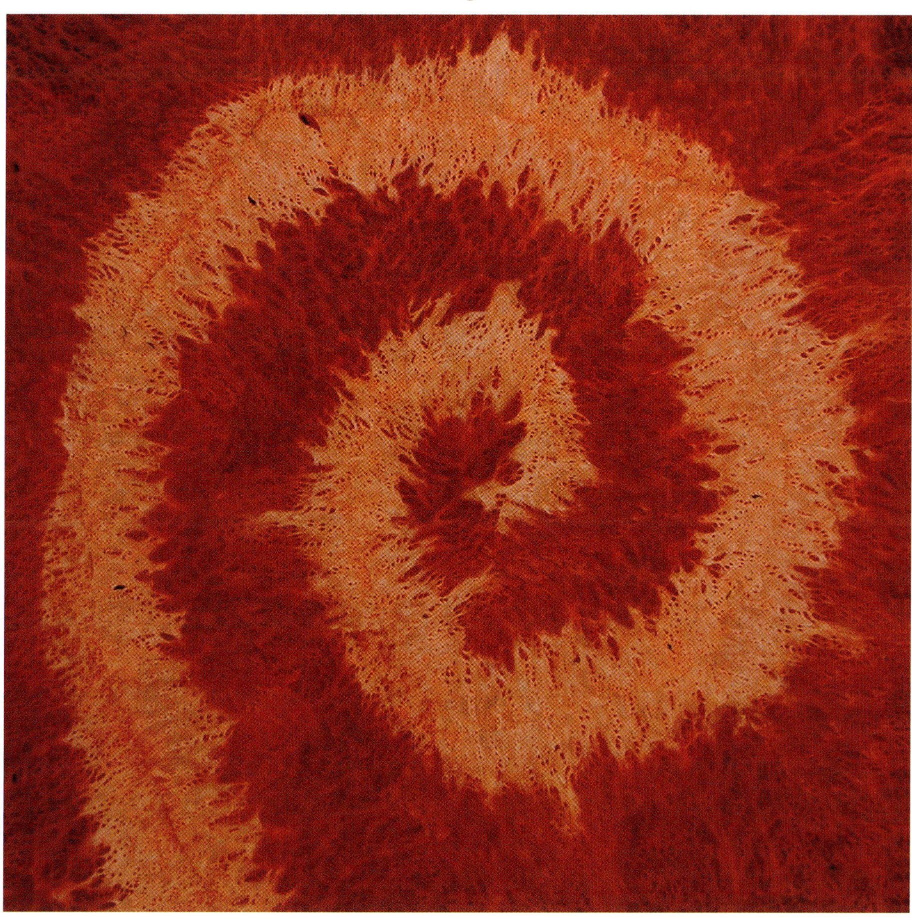

SPIRAL MATCH: see Chapter 11.

Let's Have Some Fun

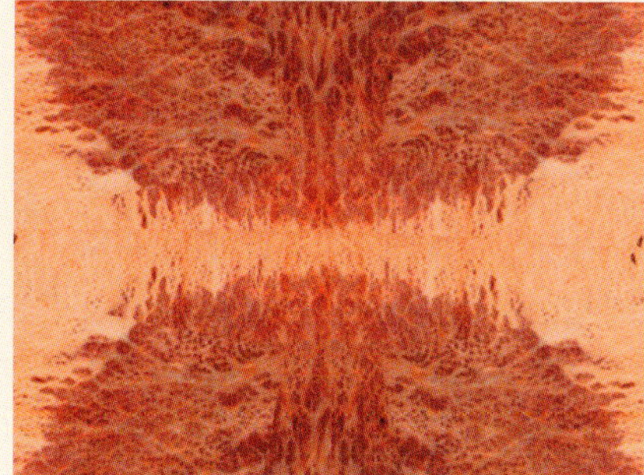

By combining a series of curved sections, complete arches can be created. (Starting to see options?)

Hand

Symmetrical heart

Asymmetrical heart

Ying-yang

6
Layout Techniques

A few techniques are available to help visualize these matches. For book matching, a mirror helps to locate the symmetrical mirrored patterns. With asymmetrical patterns it gets a bit trickier. Tracing paper, photograph collages and digital programs can help, although I prefer to simply go for it. It's relatively simple to do once matching techniques are mastered.

For book matching, you can easily see the mirrored match by holding the mirror to the veneer. With every slight movement of the mirror, the patterns change and you can spend hours visualizing the endless pattern possibilities. The veneer seam is where the mirror touches the veneer. Once you find a pattern you like, use the mirror edge to identify the exact seam location.

For two-piece book matching, use a mirror to help you visualize and locate the seam. Use the mirror as a straight edge and draw the seam line on one leaf of veneer.

For a radial match, it can get tricky when determining the size and how many pie sections you need. As you move further away from the center, the wider the pie wedges get and eventually they will be wider than the veneer leaf. If the mirrors extend off the maximum width of the veneer leaf, then either decrease the angle to increase the number of pie sections OR widen the leaves, typically with a book match.

First, if you are book matching or seaming with straight seams, it is best to divide the circle into an even number of sections such as 6, 8, 10, 12, 16, etc. (more on this later on page 83). With this even-numbered sectioning, it is easiest to use drafting triangles to define the angle of the mirrors.

For example:

- The angle is 60 degrees for a six-piece match.
- The angle is 45 degrees for an eight-piece match.
- The angle is 30 degrees for a twelve-piece match and so on.

If pre-made triangles are unavailable in non-standard sizes, you can make your own. Use these triangles to set the angle of the mirrors to easily show the true pattern.

You can spend a lot of time exploring the patterns with each subtle move of the mirror, very much like viewing a kaleidoscope. Be warned: This can bring back some flashbacks from the 1970s. Here I see a skull (I miss Jerry Garcia).

FOR A FOUR SQUARE MATCH, hold two mirrors at ninety degrees to see the entire pattern. See page 87 for final lay up.

FOR RADIAL MATCHES, hold two mirrors hinged together with tape. This helps define a pie shape and size, and shows the full sunburst pattern in the center.

Radial Matching: Tricks of the Trade

Here is a nice trick to make radial assembly easier with straight seams.

Since veneer is wood and wood is constantly moving (expanding and contracting), wedge pieces will not remain true when it is time to assemble them.

Cutting a perfect 60-degree pie slice is one thing, but by the time you start taping them all together, the total sum of the angles (which needs to be exactly 360 degrees) may be slightly smaller or larger, which can wreak havoc. The entire piece can end up in a cone form, pointing up or down.

To compensate for this movement, it is easier to tape together two half sets of the radial first (two 180 degree sections), re-cut the final seam, and then tape the two halves together. Leave the two end pieces of each half long to compensate for the final cut. See drawing.

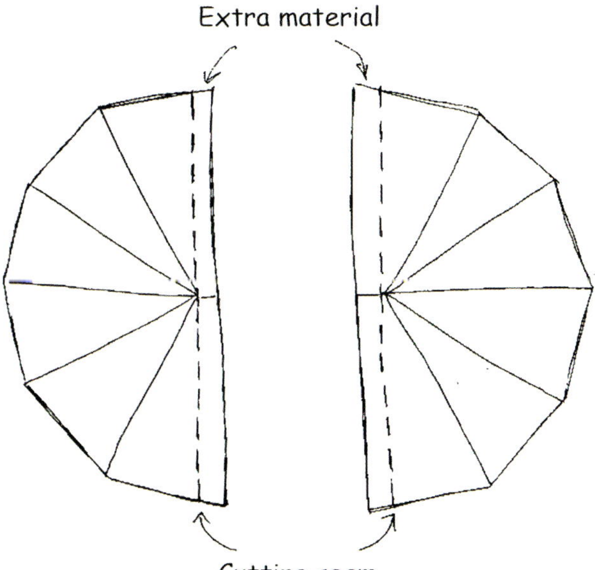

Leaving extra material on the end leaves of each half of the radial sequence is the secret to obtaining a perfect final seam.

Sequencing a Radial

Sequencing the leaves in a radial design or any multiple leaf match can be tricky in two ways: aligning the sequence order and considering the orientation of the compressed and stretched faces.

First, let's review the ramifications of the leaf sequence order.

In a 12-piece radial match, twelve, 30 degree, pie-shaped leaves make up 360 degrees of the circle. If these are matched in sequence 1 through 12 around the pie, leaf 1 matches leaf 2, 2 with 3 and so on, and 12 ends up next to 1. At that seam, the grain match or alignment would have the most grain drift difference and be very noticeable. See page 26 for drift and shift.

To alleviate this misalignment, the leaves need to be staggered around the pie; alternate the leaves so the difference between the sequence orders is equalized. See drawing.

In addition, light reflects differently off compressed and stretched faces, and it can make each surface look lighter or darker relative to the other. This effect, called chatoyance, is also enhanced by the viewing angle. When creating a radial or multi-piece match, the goal is to alternate these faces to create an even rhythm and avoid potential dark or light groupings.

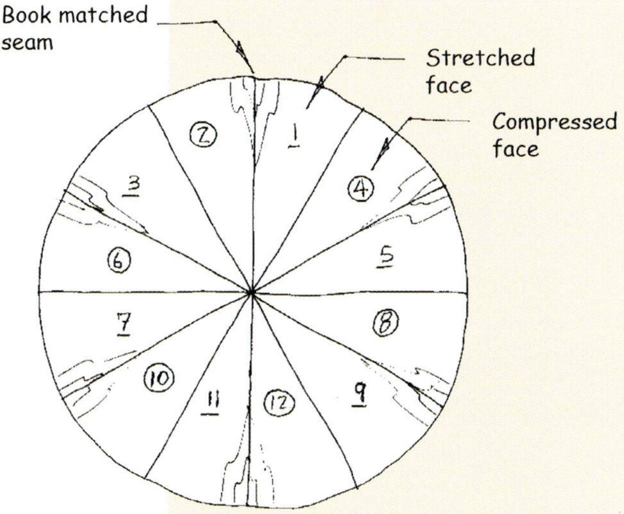

Orientations of the compressed and stretched faces.

Chatoyance is commonly seen in mahogany as the wood often looks considerably lighter or darker when viewed from different angles. Keep this in mind when laying out a radial and avoid putting these two faces next to one another. (This is not an issue when bookmatching.)

You can keep track of this easily by numbering your leaves on both sides in sequence as described in the very beginning of this book. Identify one face with an underlined number and the other face with a circled number, and alternate these faces around the radial circle accordingly. See drawing on page 83.

It is not necessary to know exactly which face is which (stretch or compressed) as long as the face number identifications (circle or underline) alternate when next to each other. You can also alternate odd and even numbers when book matching to yield the same result. See pages 83 and 88.

A blotchy leaf pattern can occur if this sequence is not followed. Leaves should alternate: light, dark, light, dark and not light, light, dark, light, dark, dark.

I often just play with the veneer and see what type of pattern it might offer me. I flip flop them around and look for unique patterns.

You can use chatoyance as a creative element. In the above dining room table, I've rotated each piece of the Avodire 30 degrees to each other to enhance this effect.

Book and Spin Match Examples

Using two leaves of highly figured Walnut, I look for options in composition.

I first check out the symmetrical book match.

Then I'll turn the one leaf 180 degree for a spin match.

The spin match is more appealing to me.

Two examples of different matches using the same leaves: a spin on the left, book match on the right. The spin match is book matched on the short ends.

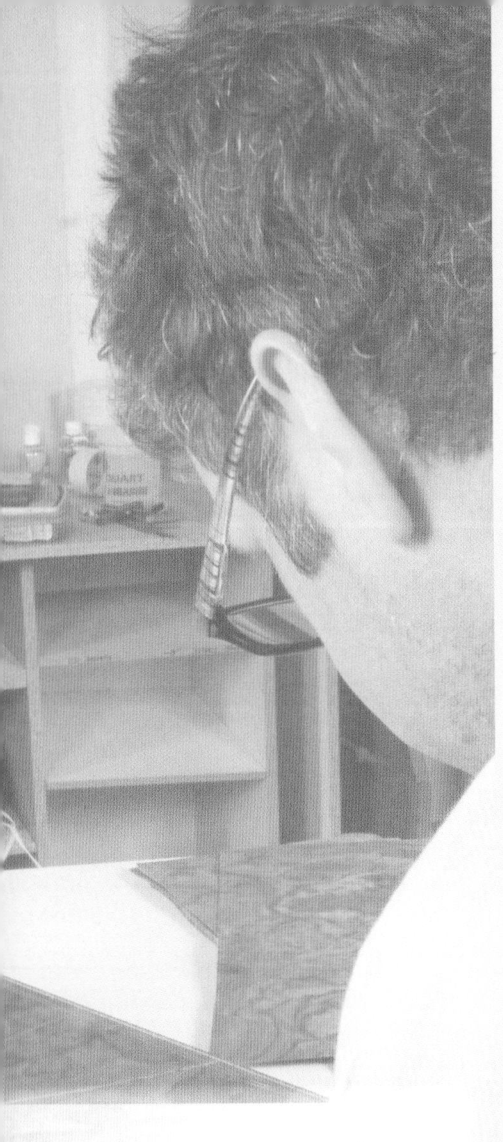

7
Straight Seaming

For nearly 5000 years veneer has been joined together with a straight seam. This straight cut can be performed by a variety of methods. I will review alternatives to a straight seam in the following chapters, but first, let's cover different ways to cut a simple book matched straight seam.

If you haven't already done so before flattening, label the front and back of each leaf in sequence (hopefully you kept them in order, pre-numbered and/or didn't erase them during the flattening process).

Label each leaf in sequence as they come off the pack as described in Chapter 2. I number both sides to help me keep track of the compressed and stretched sides (face-up and face-down sides) and I distinguish each by circling the number on the compressed sides and underlining the number on the stretched side. Be consistent.

NOTE:
For labeling and marking lines, I use a water-soluble pencil lead for easy removal. These pencils can be found in a local art store. Oil-based or graphite lead can be difficult to erase or remove before finishing.

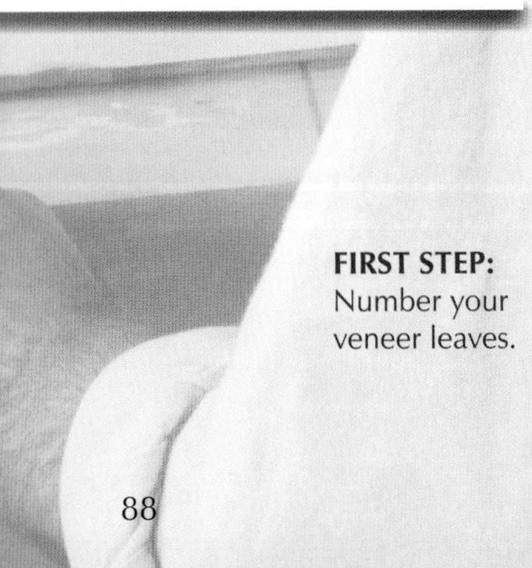

FIRST STEP: Number your veneer leaves.

These reference numbers help keep track of the faces on complex lay ups, for example, when book matching around a radial layout.

There are three general methods used to cut veneer: one sheet at a time, multiple leaves in a stack, or two leaves at a time when overlapping each other.

Stack cutting is what the term implies: all the leaves are stacked in one pile, pinched between two boards essentially making them a single block of wood, and the stack is cut all at once, usually with a power tool.

Overlap cutting is also what the term implies: two sheets are placed face-up, overlapped and cut at the same time by hand (a knife or saw) or a power tool, usually a scroll saw. This method is the basis of my wavy contour seam that I cover in Chapter 9. I review stack cutting techniques later in this chapter, too.

Let's review single leaf cutting for a two-piece book match. Each leaf is cut one at a time from the face-up side.

NOTE: Although it is desirable to have the finish surface compression-side up, this is not possible in most multi-piece lay ups as they typically involve book matching.

Seam Aligning Methods

In a book match, it is important that the seam falls exactly in the same place on each veneer leaf so the grain pattern aligns and mirrors perfectly.

First, establish the seam line, using a mirror to visualize the location. This line needs to be transferred to the back side of the matching leaf as this second leaf is flipped over for the book match. Each leaf is cut from the same face-up side.

This line transfer can be easily done in one of two ways. The simplest way is to orient and stack the leaves together and transfer the top leaf seam line around the edges to the bottom sheet. This works only if the leaves are roughly the same size.

In some cases this process is not possible as the leaves may be random in size as shown in Chapter 11.

A second method is to use the grain as a reference to locate the line, demonstrated below.

A perfectly mirrored book match can be simply achieved by marking each leaf with cutting lines on the face-up side aligned through the same grain patterns. This method is best used for precise registration of single leaf cutting and is also used in the wavy contour seam discussed in Chapter 9.

After the initial line is established, locate a significant pattern in the grain such as a knot and measure to the seam line. Here I use my grandfather's drafting dividers.

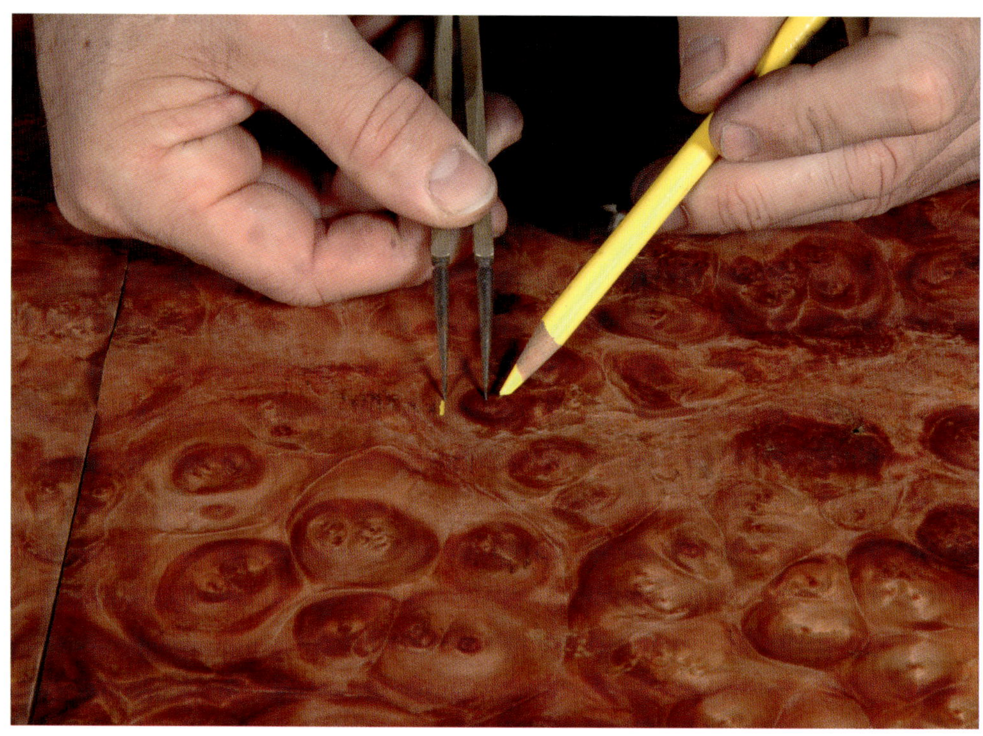

Locate the same grain spot on the back side of the matching leaf and mark your measured distance. Note that the measurement will be in the opposite direction.

Repeat this marking process in two locations to obtain the second cut line on the back side of the matching leaf.

Veneer Cutting Methods

I do most of my single cuts with a utility knife, which is beveled on both sides, so the cut creates a V-shape. If the blade is held perpendicular to the veneer the center of the cut will be slightly away from the straightedge. This can cause a problem on curved and precise alignment cutting.

To avoid this, angle the blade so the knife bevel is perpendicular to the veneer. I do this by feel as I align the blade bevel on the straight edge guide.

Also, whenever possible, place the straight edge on the good side of the veneer. This protects the veneer because if the blade wanders off the straight edge, it wanders into the "waste" side. The waste will also be the side that the utility knife blade compresses, since the blade will be angled in that direction. (See drawing below.)

Lastly, utility knives do not create kerfs or remove any material. A utility knife compresses the veneer on the top face during cutting (see drawing). In my experience this slight compression can be helpful in obtaining a tight seam as the compressed veneer expands from moisture while taping the seam or during the gluing process.

A NOTE ON WHICH FACE TO CUT: Face-up or face-down? There are arguments to be made for both, but I have found there isn't much of a difference. I typically work face-up to avoid having to think upside down and backward on complex patterns. In some cases, if there is a lot of veneer tape built up on the face-up side, I cut from the back so I can observe a critical alignment.

For small projects of two to four leaves, I cut them by hand, one at a time, face-up, simply using a utility knife or veneer saw.

I like using a heavy duty utility knife, the type with metal reinforced blade guides (yellow knife on left), snapping off the dull blade often to reveal a new sharp tip.

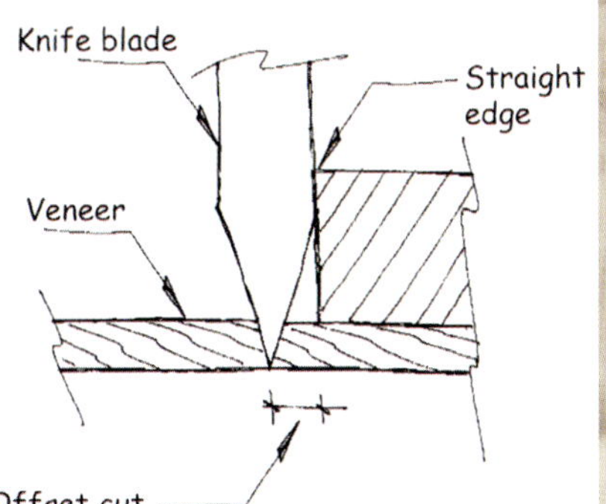

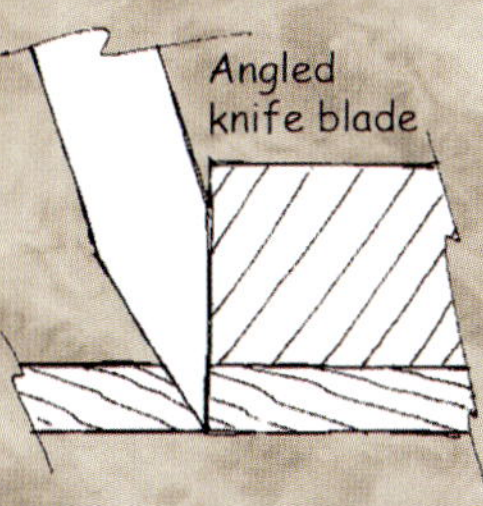

The proper alignment of the utility knife.

How to Sharpen a Veneer Saw

When a veneer saw is purchased new it is not ready for use and must be properly sharpened. Although I often use a utility knife with snap-off blades for quick "sharpening," a veneer saw has its place and purpose, such as cutting very brittle veneer. I prefer to sharpen my saws with a bevel on one face only, which allows me to perform a precise cut that is flush against my straight edge. Sharpen a new saw as follows:

Remove the veneer saw blade from the handle and clamp in a vise. Lightly file the teeth with a fine flat file to even the tips of the teeth.

With a fine triangular file, file each tooth to a point.

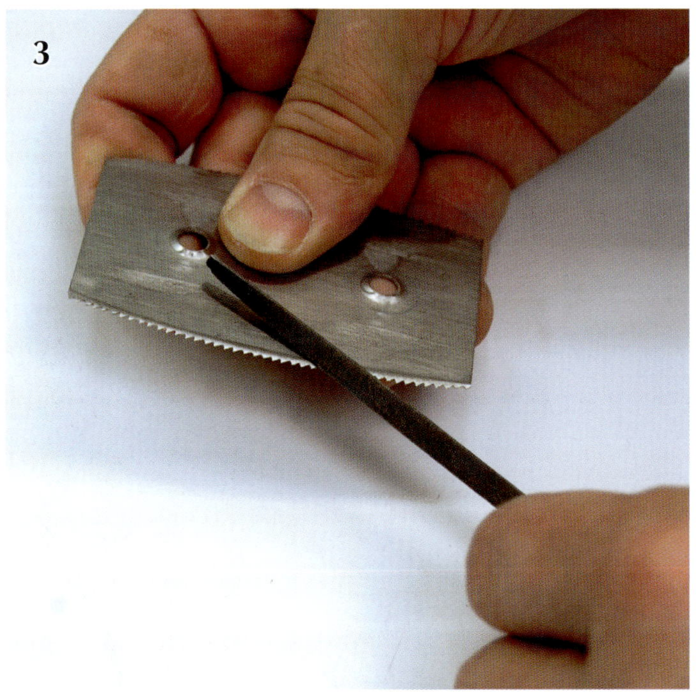

File a slight bevel on one side only (the side towards the handle when assembled). File the thickness of the blade down to a beveled edge and now each tooth tip will be a fine point.

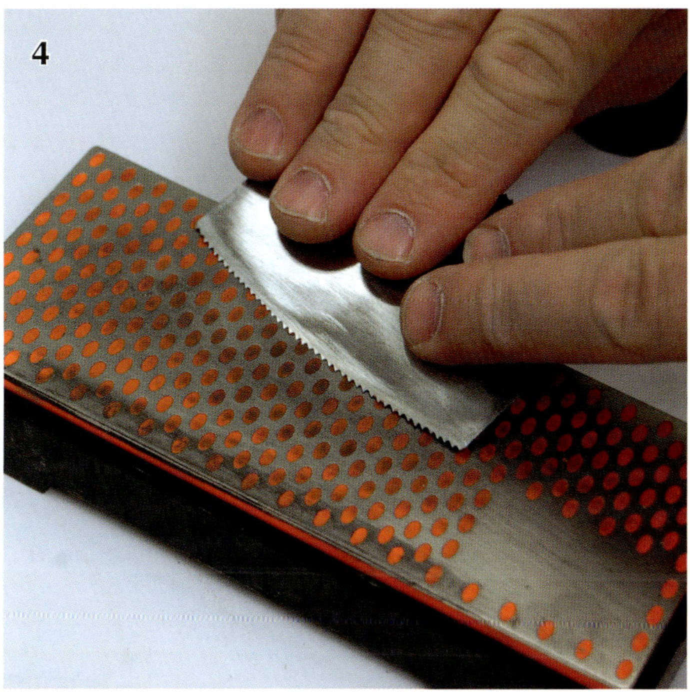

4

Hone the bevel so it is razor sharp.

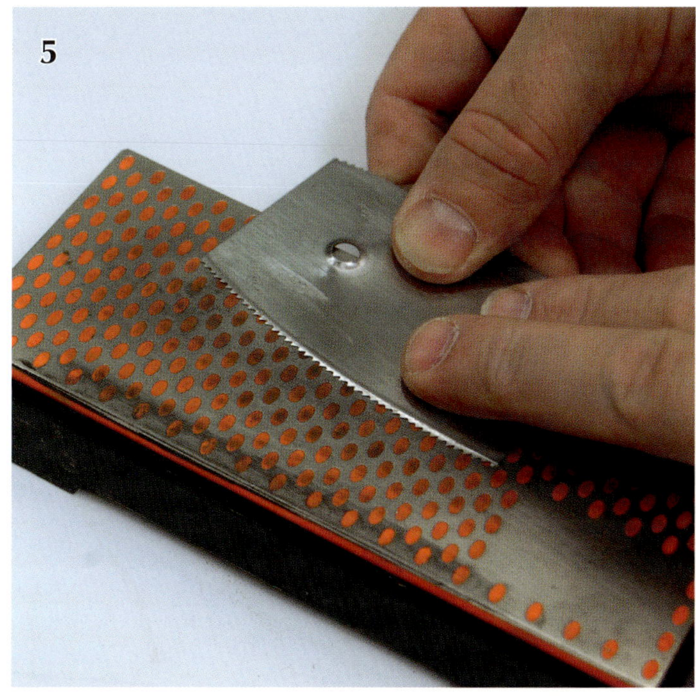

5

Flatten the back side of the blade to remove any filing burrs and refine the razor edge (very much like sharpening a chisel). Note the bevel edge.

6

Reattach the blade to the handle.

7

When assembled, the flat side will run flush (tight) against your straight edge and give you a clean cut.

Multi-Leaf Cutting

For multiple leaf jobs, veneer leaves can be cut in a group or stack. Below are a variety of methods of stack cutting, but universally there are fundamental considerations that help cuts go more smoothly.

1. Conditioned (flattened/softened) veneer makes cutting veneer dramatically easier.
2. Using a perfectly straight cutting edge or shooting board is a must. Any slight bow in the cutting edge (and subsequently the cut veneer) will be magnified as the leaves are book matched.
3. It is critical to press the stacked leaves tightly together, essentially making them into a single block of wood.
4. Use a sharp cutting blade to help prevent chipping of the veneer.
5. Use a top and bottom "waste" piece of veneer (I use poplar) to help prevent chip-outs.
6. Align the grain pattern between each leaf to ensure a symmetrical and matched pattern.

Add a registration mark on each leaf to help alignment.

By slightly shifting the veneer at the end, I can see and align the grain. I use an office stapler, pins, spring clamps or tape to hold the aligned leaves together while pressing between two "shooting" boards before cutting. A shooting board is a straight edge used to guide my cutting tool.

Aligning the grain at each end is a must.

Cutting Methods

Depending on the species and condition of the veneer, some methods simply won't work. It is important to master a variety of them to accommodate various scenarios.

Router

After tightly clamping the stack of veneer flat between two shooting boards, I use a pattern maker's router bit to make the cut. A pattern bit is a flush cutting bit with the bearing on top, which is guided by the top straight shooting board.

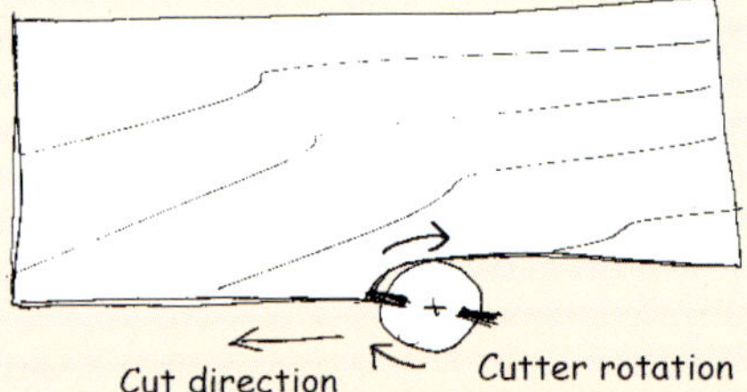

For a clean cut, perform a climb cut to trim the veneer straight. A climb cut runs the router *with* the rotation of the bit, like a wheel running along the road, which is opposite to a typical cut that moves the router against the rotation of the bit.

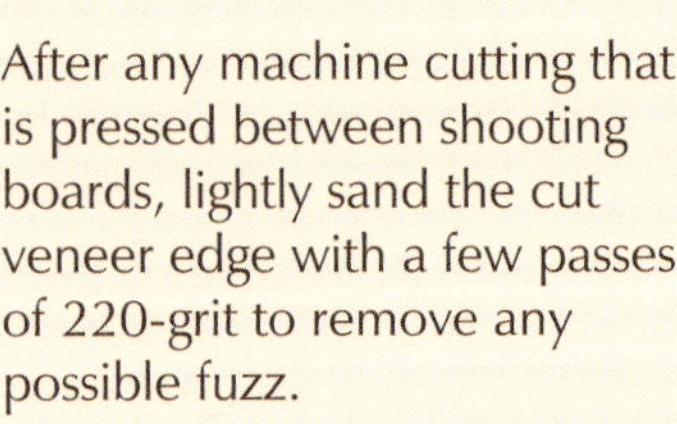

After any machine cutting that is pressed between shooting boards, lightly sand the cut veneer edge with a few passes of 220-grit to remove any possible fuzz.

Another method to obtain a straight "cut" is to sand the stack of veneer on a *straight* straight-edged sander.

Sander

This method works only if the veneer is flat and doesn't require clamping as the clamps will get in the way of the table bed. If the veneer is flat, hand pressure will do. It is possible to screw or bolt the boards together.

Joiner

A joiner will also produce a good straight edge. This method can be performed with a single board to hold the veneer against the fence (as shown) or clamping between two boards. This method is not accurate for hitting a specific line.

Hand Plane

The veneer stack has to be first roughly cut (typically by a veneer saw) then planed straight on the shooting boards. Note: The bottom edge of the plane, not the blade, runs along the shooting edge below the veneer to guide the cut. Here, boards are used to press the veneer flat by cauls wedging them to the ceiling. This system works great for all types of clamping, only if you have low ceilings.

An old school method uses a finely tuned and sharp plane to "shoot" a straight seam.

Guillotines

Guillotines are used in production shops for high volume slicing. Paper cutters (guillotines) work great too.

Table Saw

With two plywood cauls hand pressed or screwed together, a table saw can work well to cut a stack of veneer. It helps to have a negative rake saw blade.

Sliding Table Saw

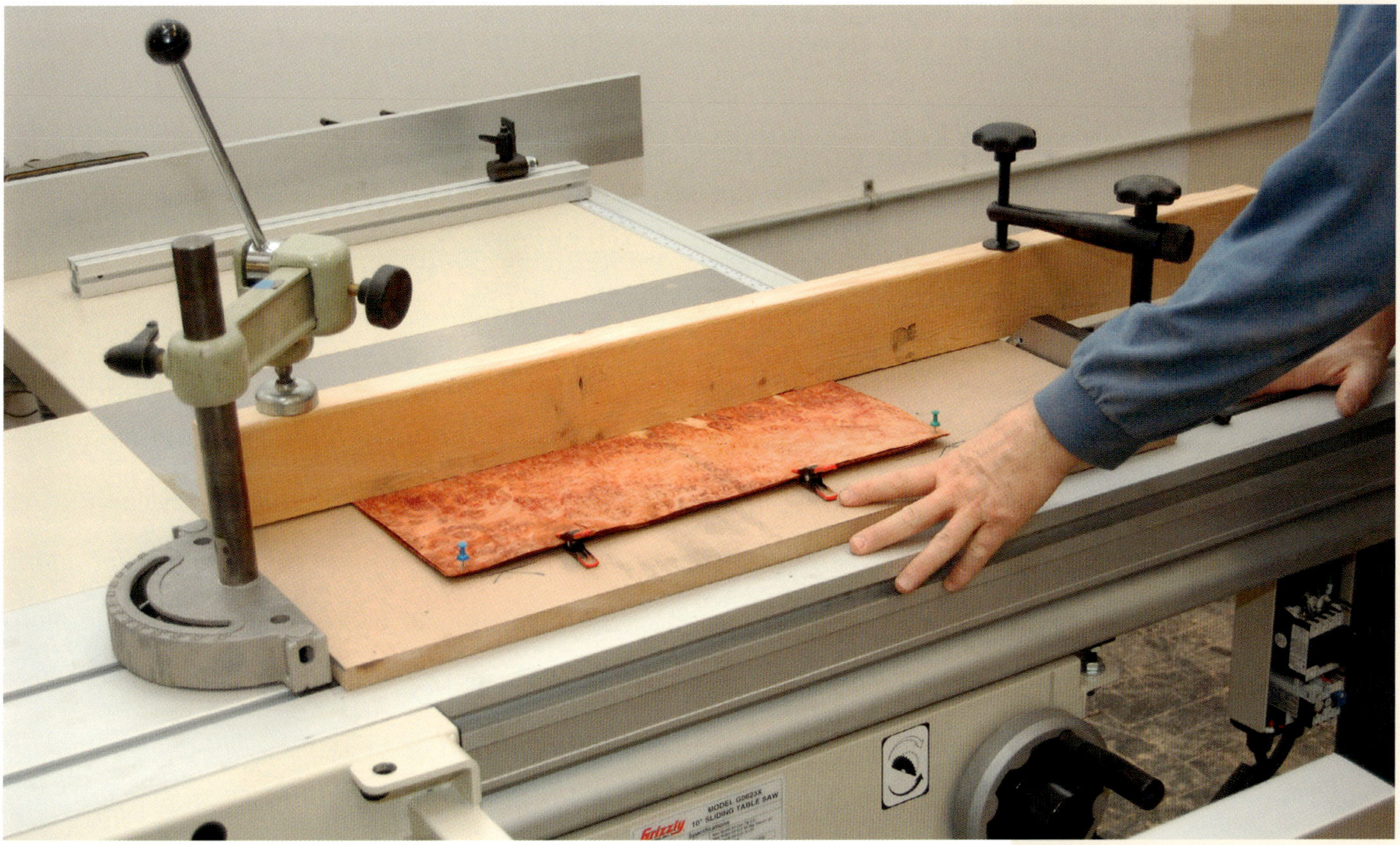

Clamping the veneer on a sliding table saw works well. A slightly bowed clamping caul compensates for any deflection in a long board because clamping is done only at each end.

8
Taping

This sounds simple, but **DON'T SKIP THIS CHAPTER.**

After a veneer seam has been precisely cut it needs to be joined together and held firmly in place until it is pressed to a substrate. This can be achieved using a few methods such as edge gluing, stitching and taping.

With taping as the preferred method of seaming, two types of tape can be used: masking tape or veneer tape.

While masking tape is great to use for temporarily holding seams together, it has some major pitfalls if used while pressing the veneer. It is too thick; it can leave an impression in the veneer during pressing; the adhesive can leave a sticky residue on the surface; and, the most irritating problem, it is extremely difficult to remove after pressing. Because of these factors, I avoid using masking tape to secure the seam together for pressing.

Veneer tape is a thin paper tape with a water-activated adhesive on one side. The tape is dampened to activate the adhesive and applied to the two-piece seam, taping them together. More on this process further in this chapter.

Veneer tape comes in two major types: perforated and non-perforated, in a number of widths and thicknesses, and in two colors.

Perforated tape has holes in the thin tape which makes removing the tape easier IF you are sanding it off (less tape, less to remove). If you are scraping the tape off, I have found that it tears up into smaller pieces making it more difficult to remove. Another advantaged is that the holes allow you to see through the tape at the seam.

One fallacy is that perforated tape can be used on the bottom of veneer and glued between the veneer and the substrate, trapping it in the glue line forever. This is NOT true. Never leave the tape in the glue line, never, never, never.

Non-perforated tape is stronger, easier to apply, is less fragile, and easier to remove. (See page 107 for removal.)

Properties Of Veneer Tape:

• Weight: heavy (thicker) tape is easier to handle and remove (See page 107) but that extra thickness can build up with multiple layers and leave a depression in softer veneers.

• Width: It doesn't really matter which width you use. I like to use 1" wide tape. It has enough gluing surface to grab (glue) the veneer together and hold it in place. The wider the tape, the easier it is to use on a wavy contour seam. See Chapter 9.

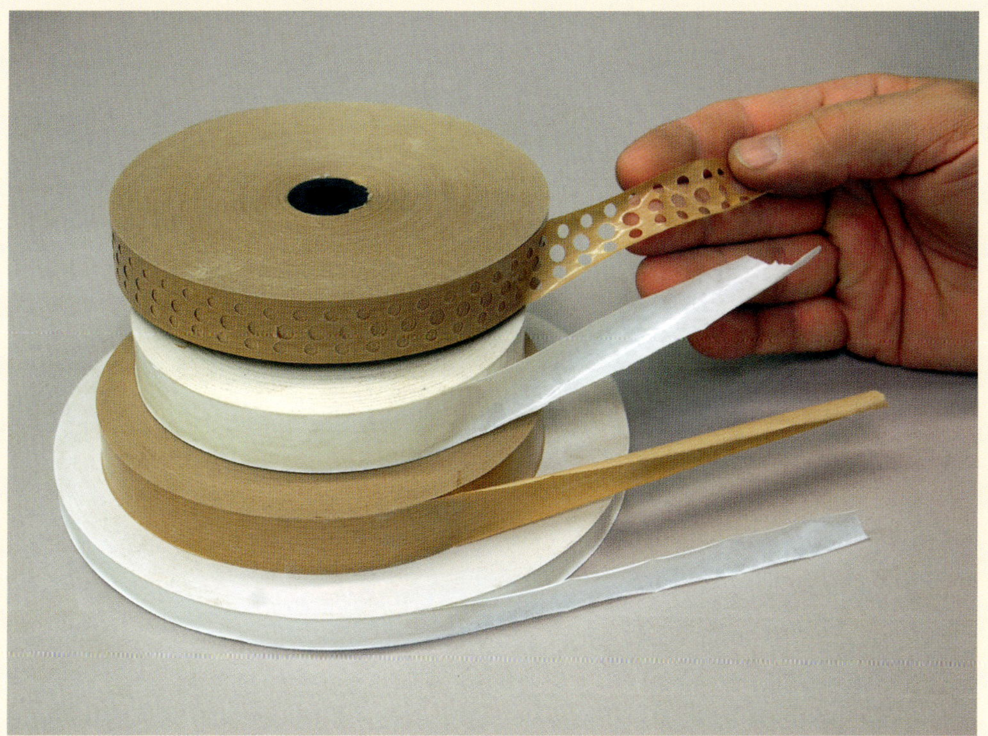

The most common styles of veneer tape are (top to bottom): Perforated, 1″ width, 34 gram (thickness) craft paper tape, referred to as "perf" tape; Non-perforated, 1″ width, 34 gram white cellulose paper tape; Non-perforated, 1″ width, 40 gram craft paper tape, referred to as "non-perf", the extra thickness adds strength; Non-perforated, .5″ width, 34 gram white cellulose paper tape (I use this for small intricate multiple-piece marquetry.

NOTE: In some instances the veneer can be seamed during the gluing process such as in hot hide gluing. In the majority of veneering that involves multiple pieces, usually the veneer pieces are fastened together in a "sketch face" to create a single layer sheet, and then pressed as one piece. At the end of this Chapter, I briefly cover other methods of seam joining.

Color: I prefer white tape so I can see through it to locate intersecting seams. You can also see through it to locate intersecting seams. Tan tape is typically heavier and stronger; I use this tape only on unruly burl that has not been conditioned.

Tape Application

It is not necessary to tape across or perpendicular to the seam (more on this later). There is enough adhesive on 1″ wide tape to hold the veneer together. Adding three more inches when taping perpendicular to the seam is just wasting tape and increasing removal time.

Wider tape also makes gluing the wavy contour seam easier as you are taping curves together. The wider the tape the more curve is covered in a single straight piece of tape.

I've seen many professional craftsman use two hands to tear off a piece of tape, moisten with a dampened sponge, and apply to the veneer. On complex lay-ups, hundreds of pieces of tape are used, and I think it is a huge waste of time. It's a messy method that allows adhesive to get all over your fingers and slows the entire process down.

The most efficient way of taping is to invest in a veneer tape dispenser and/or make one. Modifying a masking tape dispenser with a sponge or by adding a postage stamp licker also works.

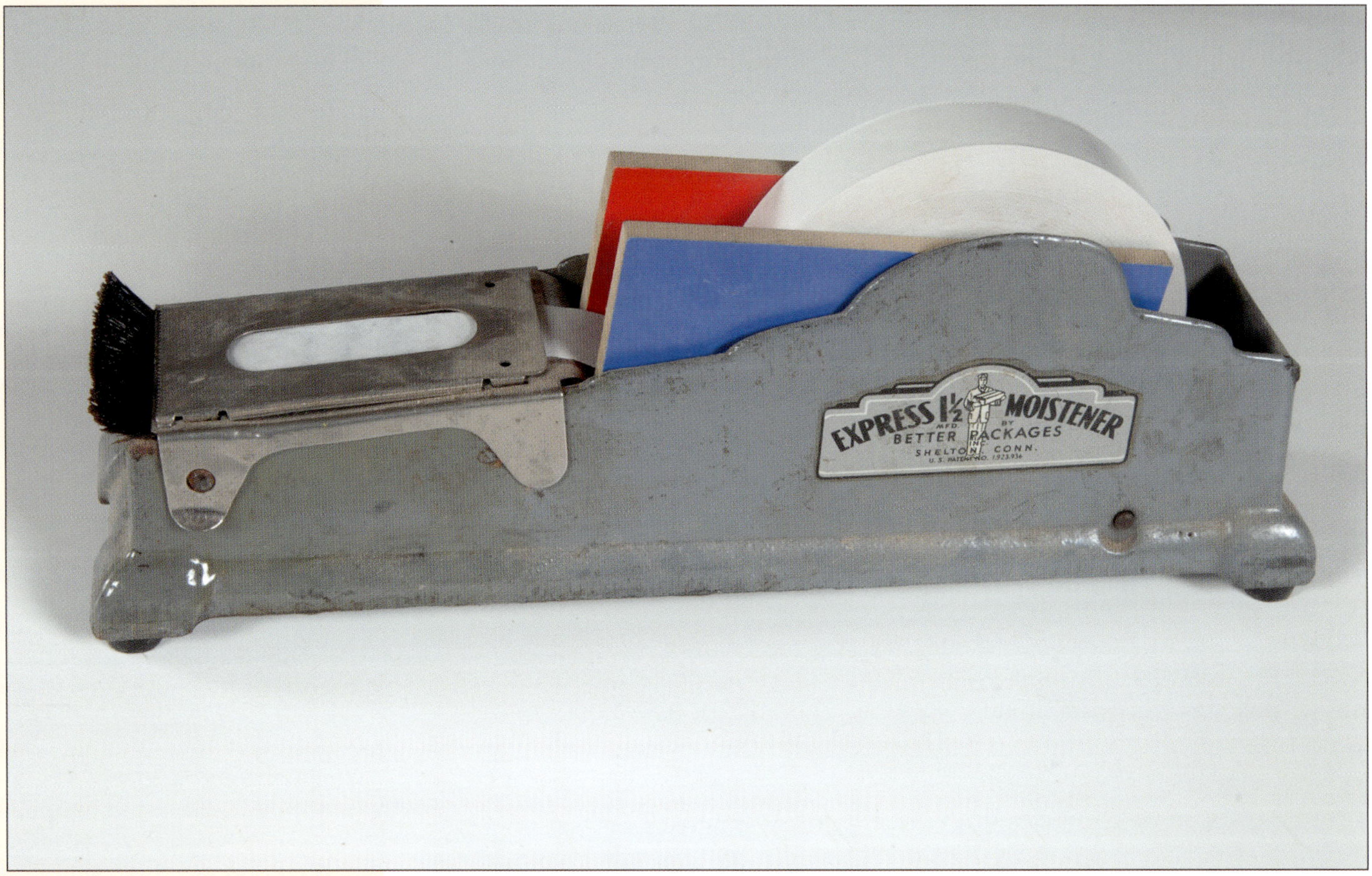

A professional veneer tape dispenser has a reservoir of water with a brush that soaks up the water and dampens the tape. A slot before the brush allows you to advance the tape and has a serrated edge to cleanly tear off the piece. This is especially great for long lengths of tape, and you can do this with one hand.

Distilled water ensures that no mineral deposits will stain your wood. If your water is hard or comes from a well, use distilled water. An old iron (or an excuse to buy a new one) will help set the tape in the next step.

Setting The Tape

When taping a seam with veneer tape, remember you are adding moisture to the veneer through the moistened tape, so the veneer will swell slightly at the joint, making the seam appear nice and tight for the moment. So, as the tape dries, it shrinks and pulls the seam together. Some species of wood will expand more than the tape shrinks, which causes the seam to open as the wood continues to dry and shrink after the tape has dried.

To avoid this, use a household iron set on medium heat, steam off. Iron the tape to set the glue and remove excess moisture that might have been absorbed into the veneer. This sets the glue immediately and prevents any veneer slippage. If the tape is left wet, slippage can occur until the veneer adhesive dries.

This ironing process is not like ironing a shirt: The steam setting should be off, and you should use only the tip of the iron. If you use the entire face of the iron you can over-dry the veneer and cause it to shrink, warp, and curl. Use just the tip of the iron and make one or two quick, light passes over the tape, pushing down firmly. This will set the adhesive and remove excess moisture. Small veneering, quilting, or travel irons work great too.

I've seen many people temporarily tape with masking tape first then apply the veneer tape while removing the masking tape as they go. Unless the veneer is extremely gnarly and wrinkled, this is a wasted step. Simply tack the veneer with small pieces of veneer tape and then tape over the entire seam with more veneer tape. It is OK to have two or three layers of veneer tape built up.

I've also seen people work from the back side, taping with masking tape, then flipping the entire sheet over, taping the face with veneer tape, then flipping again and removing the masking tape as they go. This is also a waste of time. (There are exceptions to every rule and I will explain in Chapter 11 when this flip flopping is helpful).

The reasoning for taping the back is to avoid masking tape adhesive from touching the good face and leaving residue that can inhibit the finishing process. In all my years this has never been a problem, but, of course, I thoroughly prep the face before finishing. (See page 60.)

I've also seen (and admit doing this myself) masking tape that has not been removed from the back and gluing it between the veneer and substrate, which causes all sorts of problems down the road. Some things I've had to learn the hard way.

TIP: Don't skip this section!

Tape the Seam

Carefully align the veneer grain together, working on the face-up side. Since the grain will vary slightly from leaf to leaf, first align a significant element towards the center and then check the entire seam for any drastic grain drift. You might have to split the difference to compensate for variations in the pattern.

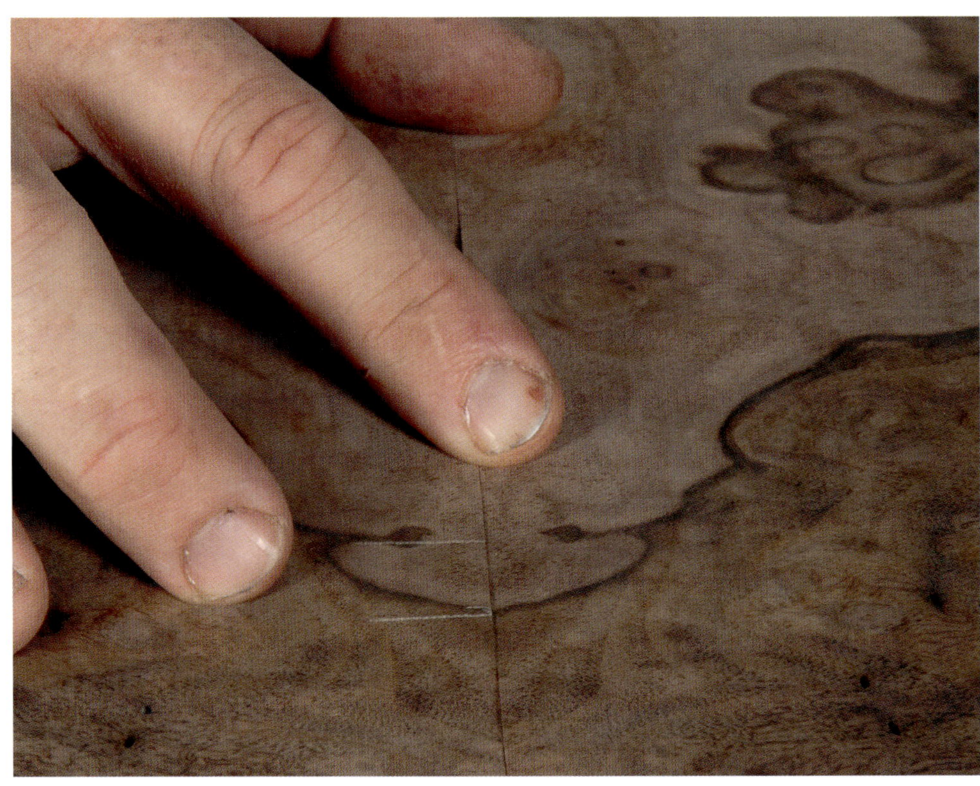

Start taping in the middle or at a significant intersection, and tack two leaves together with a single piece of tape, roughly 2″ long.

After tacking the seam in the center, work out to the edges, keeping the seam flat and flush, smoothing out any irregularities between the two sides, taping and setting with an iron as you go, every six inches or so. On nice flat veneer sometimes only three pieces of tape will do the trick: one in the center and one at each end.

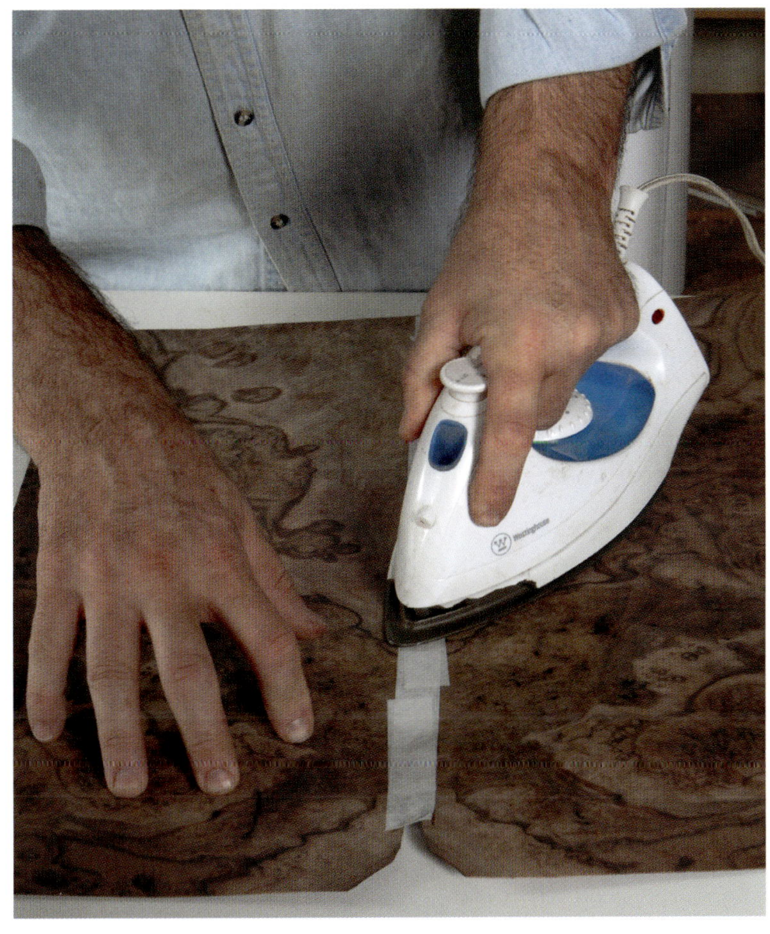

Setting the tape with an iron speeds up this process and ensures a tight and immediate seam bond.

After the tacking is complete, run a length of tape over the entire seam. It is okay to tape over the smaller tacked pieces. Do not leave any part of the seam un-taped.

Tape over any open voids and knot holes to help prevent glue from squeezing through during pressing.

On fragile veneer, if you haven't already done so, tape the entire perimeter to help prevent splitting during handling. This can be done before seaming only if you are absolutely sure which side is face-up.

Removing Veneer Tape:

After pressing, the veneer tape has to be removed by sanding, scraping or releasing the adhesive.

Since the adhesive in veneer tape is water based, it will release by simply wetting it lightly. Dampen the tape with a cloth or sponge.

Allow enough time for the water to loosen the adhesive: it can take two or three applications of water. The tape will turn clear-ish when it loosens. Simply pull the strip off. When there are two layers of tape, a second application of water may be required.

If the tape starts to fall apart, a scraper helps. Let the water do its job.

Afterwards, it is a good idea to keep the panels flat and sticker them so they can dry evenly. Stickering is when boards are raised off a surface with sticks, allowing for air circulation around both sides of the panel for even drying.

NOTE: Water can expand the veneer and create bubbles on any small areas of veneer that have not been glued down. This works for any type of glue you are using. It is better to find it now than down the road, OR in a client's house in Miami in July. Been there, done that.

I know what you might be thinking. Yikes! All that water into the wood! What about expansion or warping? If you have a good pressed panel and even if you have used PVA glue, then let the glue set overnight. If you have used resin glue this will not be a problem at all. Don't hose the panel down with water, apply only a light amount on the surface of the tape.

If I use PVA glue, I remove any glue glaze (glue that has squeezed through the veneer to the top face). A *very* light amount of water loosens the PVA glue and can be easily scrubbed off with a Scotchbright™ pad in lieu of sanding. Notice the white haze (glue glaze) that the water has revealed, at the top left of the veneer panel.

Masking Tape – Breaking Some Rules

Okay, I admit there are always situations that merit breaking my own rules.

Again, the disadvantage in using masking tape is that it is much thicker than veneer tape and can leave depressions in your veneer. The glue can also be too aggressive and very difficult to remove, especially after pressing. Sanding it off is impossible as it will gum up the paper, and scraping takes forever.

On unseen panel backs or bottoms, (or when rushing for a photo shoot), I sometimes cheat and use masking tape to seam the veneer together. Use the same aligning steps as with veneer tape.

Remove the masking tape right after pressing using an iron. The heat loosens the adhesive but still leaves a sticky residue on the surface. Mineral spirits and a scraper helps remove this goo.

Edge Gluing By Hand (This Is A Great Trick)

Tape the entire seam with masking tape as previously described, face-side up.

Face-side down, fold the seam open 90 degrees over the edge of a table and apply a bead of glue into the seam. This will be a bit messy and appears to be overkill.

Place a sheet of flexible material such as plastic laminate or 1/8″ Masonite between two benches to create a half pipe and lay the veneer face-down flat. The half pipe keeps the veneer seam aligned and flush along with the masking tape. Scrape the excess glue from the seam with a putty knife.

After fifteen minutes or so the glue will be dry, the two pieces of veneer will be edge glued together and the masking tape can be simply peeled off by hand, since it hasn't been pressed. This method works only with very flat and long material. It is by far the fastest way to join two leaves of veneer together. Production facilities use a similar process.

Production Techniques

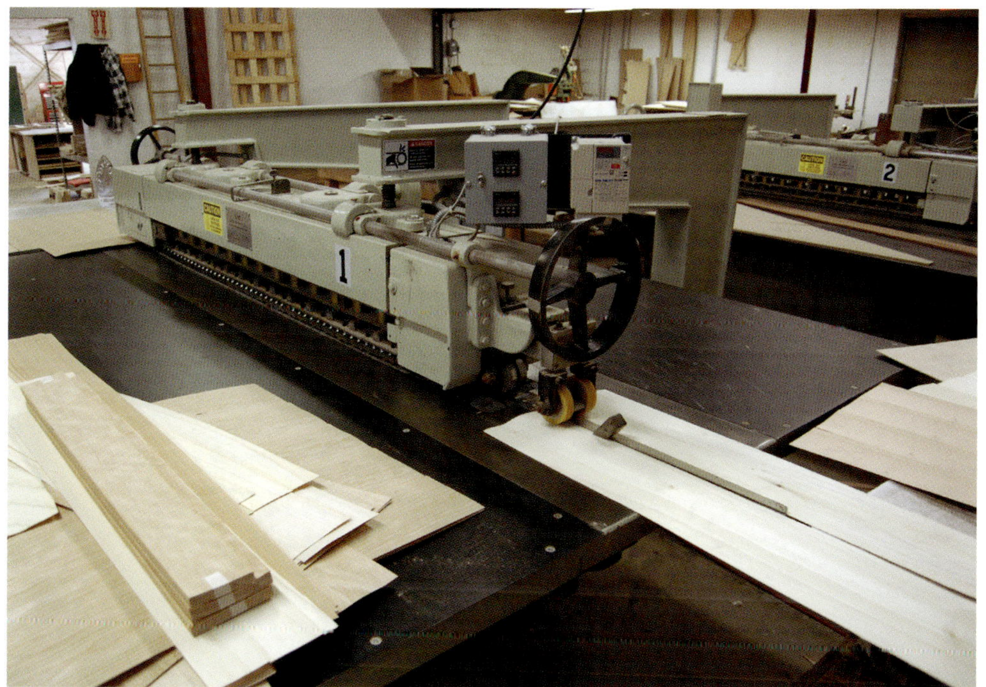

A stack of veneer edges are sprayed with heat-sensitive glue. The leaves are run through a seamer that pushes the two leaves together while applying heat and instantaneously setting the glue, joining the two leaf edges together.

A veneer stitcher is another method of quickly seaming veneer together. They can be floor-mounted or handheld (shown). It is best used for production runs on flat and long seams. Two leaves of veneer are run through the stitching machine face-up as two wheels push them together. A heated head presses a glue-impregnated string and zigzags across the seam as it passes under a pinch roller firmly securing the two together. After the veneer is pressed to a substrate the string is pulled off.

Automatic taping machines push veneer together and applies tape at the same time. They can be handheld or large floor mounted models.

9
Wavy Contour Seam

I've said it before and I'll say it again: for centuries veneer has been seamed with straight seams. Using a straight seam in burls can be very noticeable and visually distracts from the swirling grain pattern.

A wavy contour seam can be used to hide this unsightly straight line, especially in burls. This seam can be use in any type of match, and the following example is a book match using this technique.

The wavy seam is concealed by winding through, in and around the grain. The general concept is that two veneer leaves will be overlapped, oriented in the same direction (both faces up or down), the grain lined up referencing both axes, and a wavy seam is cut through both leaves at the same time, making the seam align perfectly, and becoming nearly invisible.

In lieu of a straight seam, the cut will wiggle and weave around the grain.

Working on both leaves face-side up, determine the location of the seam as described in Chapter 9. Be sure to extend the seam line to the edge of the leaves as these will be used to align the two leaves in one axis (left to right).

Draw a reference line on both leaves perpendicular to the seam. This helps align the grain in the other axis (top to bottom). Use a significant grain element such as a knot to locate this line.

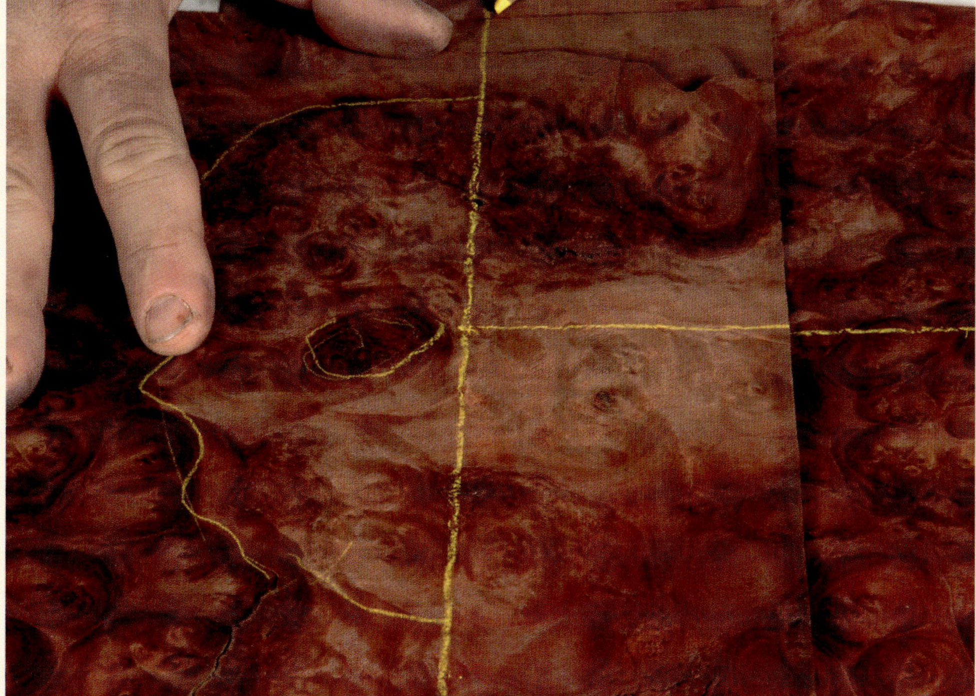

Align the two leaves of veneer to both reference lines. Note that my pencil points to the edge alignment line at the very top of this photo.

Temporarily tape the two leaves together securely with masking tape. On larger pieces, I tape both sides, the front and back.

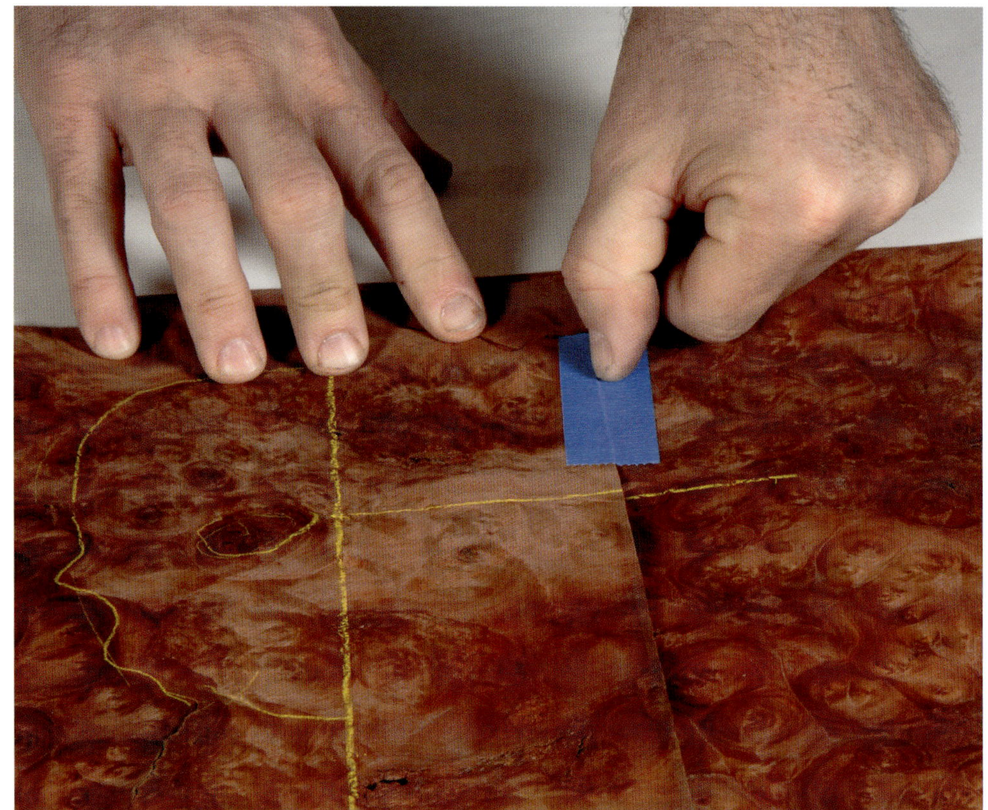

Completely tape the overlap to ensure that the two leaves won't move. Since these leaves have not been conditioned, I also taped over the seam that will be cut. **Note:** I've taped open voids as well as the entire perimeter of both leaves to prevent additional splitting during handling. This tape can be either veneer tape as shown or masking tape, as I am working on the face-up side.

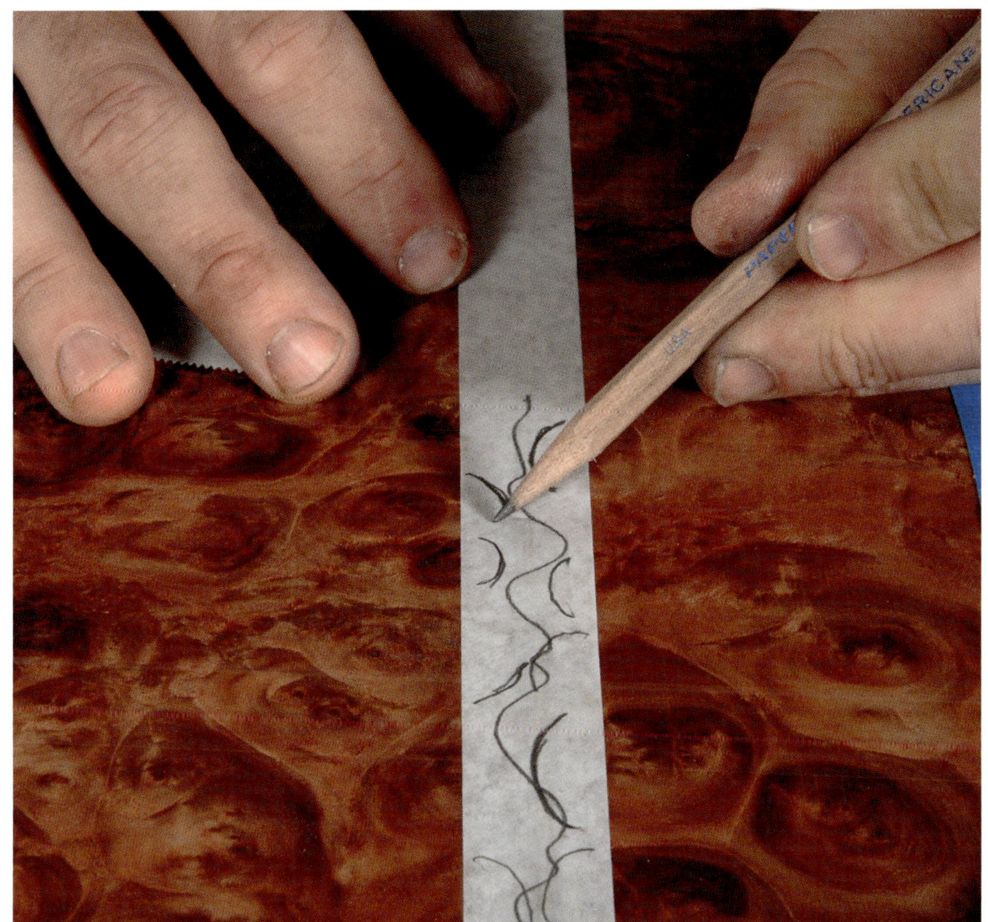

Use 34 gram white veneer tape to "see" through and determine the cutting path. Here I've sketched out the prominent figure elements to cut around.

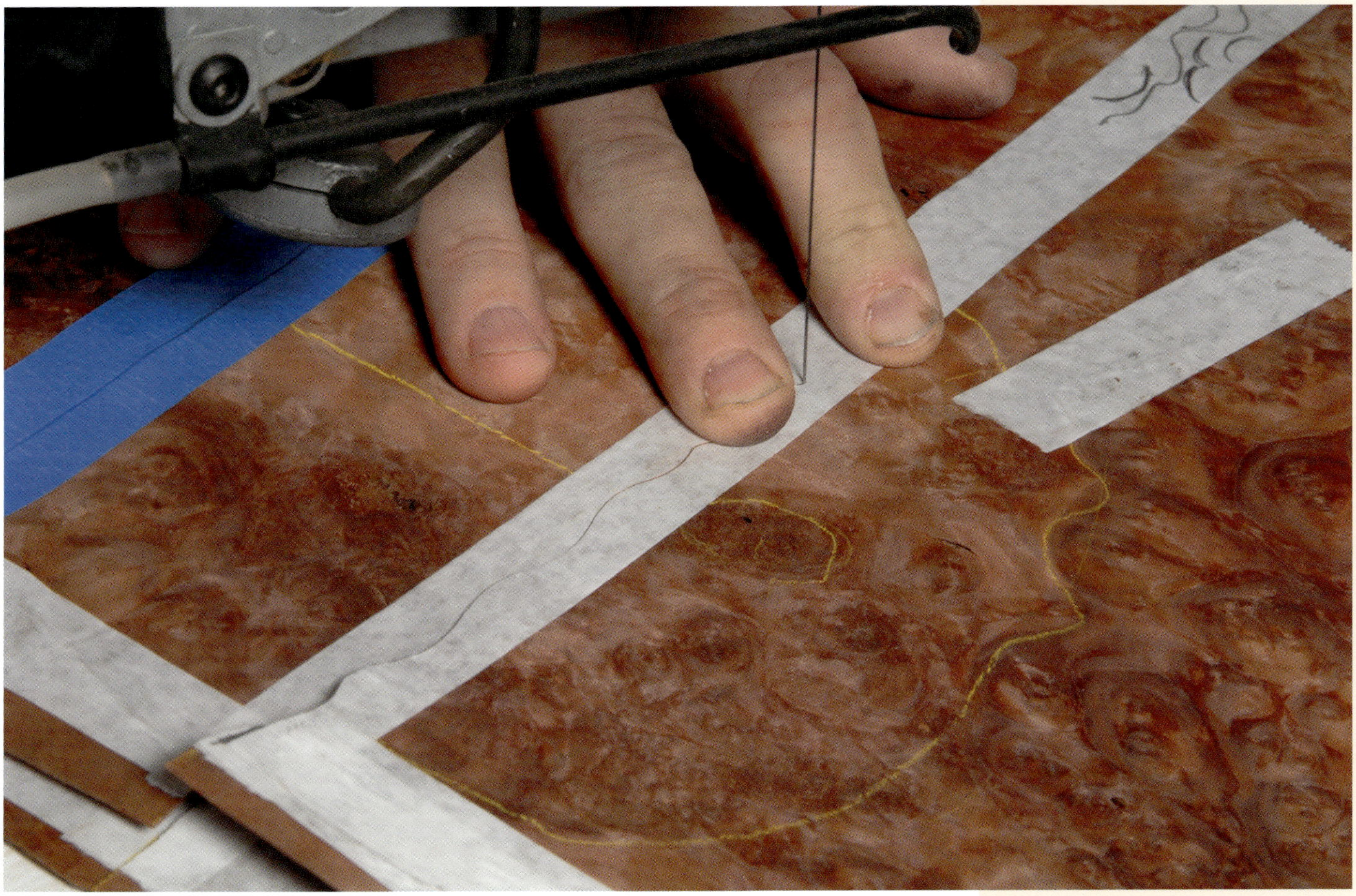

Using a scroll saw set at 14 degrees, I cut down the center of my seam line, winding through the grain pattern much like in a large repair (see Chapter 4). This is the double-bevel cut, wavy contour seam.

To help maintain a match, the width of the wave shouldn't wander more than 3/4″ back and forth (my tape is 1″ which is a helpful guide). A random squiggled cut helps conceal the seam.

Remove the overlap waste pieces.

The overlapped seam now matches perfectly. The veneer tape also helps prevent chip out while cutting.

Tape the seam together in a similar fashion as in Chapter 8. Start from the center: the two halves will self align due to the random curved seam. Work your way to the edges. Again, it is OK to tape over tape.

Remember to set the tape with an iron.

Voila! The match is mirrored and symmetrical (viewed from the back).

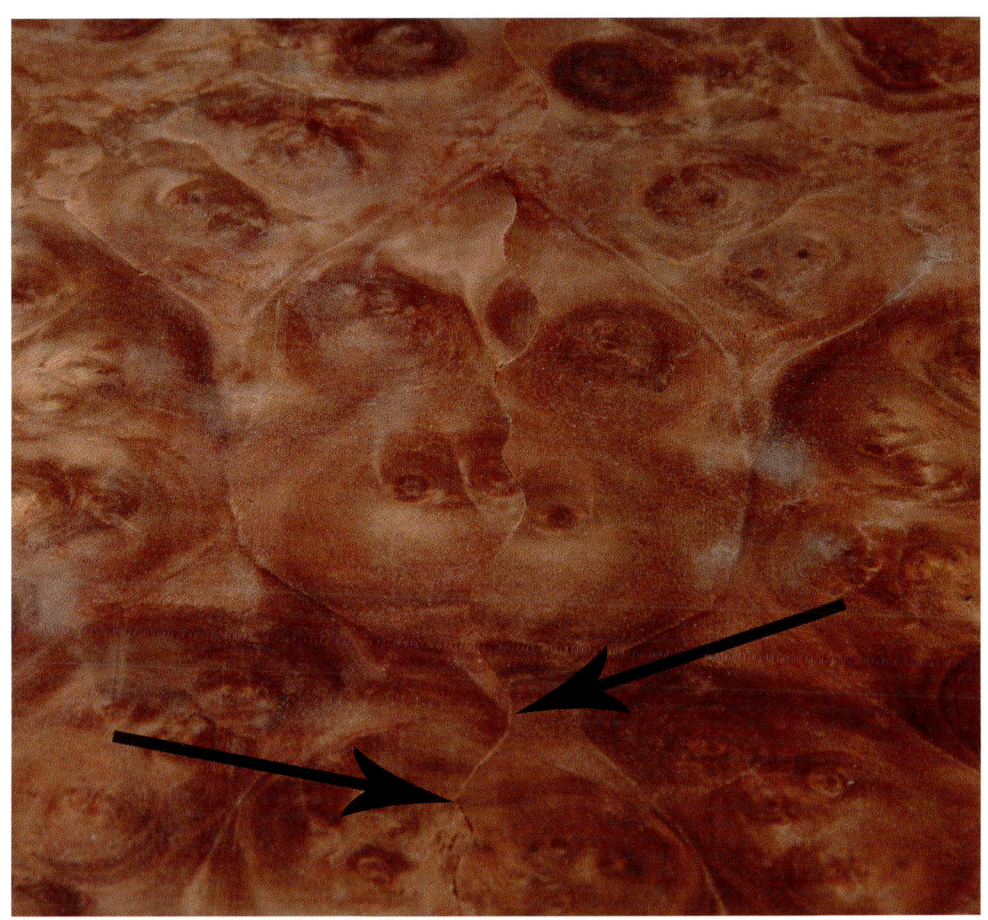

The seam is almost invisible and does not detract from the grain pattern.

The wavy contour seam can be cut by hand using a home made template. It will not have a double bevel cut.

10
Pressing

After all the hard work is done, it's time to glue the veneer to a substrate or core.

As stated in the beginning of this book, veneer has received a bad rap due to the poor substrates initially used in the 1960s and 1970s. Since then great advances have been made to these engineered boards. They now provide superior advantages over using hardwood or plywood as a substrate.

There are a few factors that determine the quality of your pressed panel: the core or sub-straight; the glue and its application; and the press.

Veneer can be glued to just about anything if you use the right of type glue. You can glue onto solid wood or engineered boards such as particle board or fiberglass composite, and clear acrylic for translucent panels.

A test is always a good idea for gluing to alternative materials and a simple thermal shock test is a good way to see if it will hold up. After gluing a small 12″ x 12″ test panel, put the panel in a refrigerator overnight, then place it in a sunny hot window the next day. Doing this a few times will stress the limits of the TEC (thermal expansion coefficient) and give you a good idea if the veneer, adhesive, and substrate are compatible and securely bonded. It is not rocket science, but this process has been useful for me.

The Core or Sub-Straight

There are many core options available, each with their own physical properties, so talking to your local rep can help you decide which is best for your particular application.

For most flat lay-ups, I use molding grade, 3/4″ thick MDF or 45-lb flake board (also known as particle or chip board). These engineered panels are dimensionally stable; they also come in a variety of sizes, densities, thicknesses, and moisture resistances. They can also be honeycomb-cored for strength and even back kerfed for flexibility.

It is important that you use furniture or cabinet-grade materials: these have higher tolerances and are made specifically for veneering.

For curved panels, I use multiple layers of 1/8″ hardboard (Masonite™) or pre-kerfed panels designed for bending.

On occasion, and when weight is a concern, I use a honeycomb-cored panel. This is a panel made with a honeycombed internal core, sandwiched between two pieces of 1/8″ Masonite™ or 1/8″ three-ply poplar plywood. These panels are extremely strong, lightweight and flat.

Lastly, creating a balanced panel is very important to help ensure that the panel stays flat. A panel that is "balanced" means it is veneered on both sides of the core with using similar veneers that are comparable in density so the two sides of the core will expand and contract at the same rate and keep the entire panel flat and stable.

The grain orientation should also run in the same direction. When working with burl, it's best to use burl on both sides, but if the back is not easily seen, then a straight-grain veneer that is similar in density will work fine, and the grain direction is not important. Be warned, if you press only one side of the panel, it WILL warp.

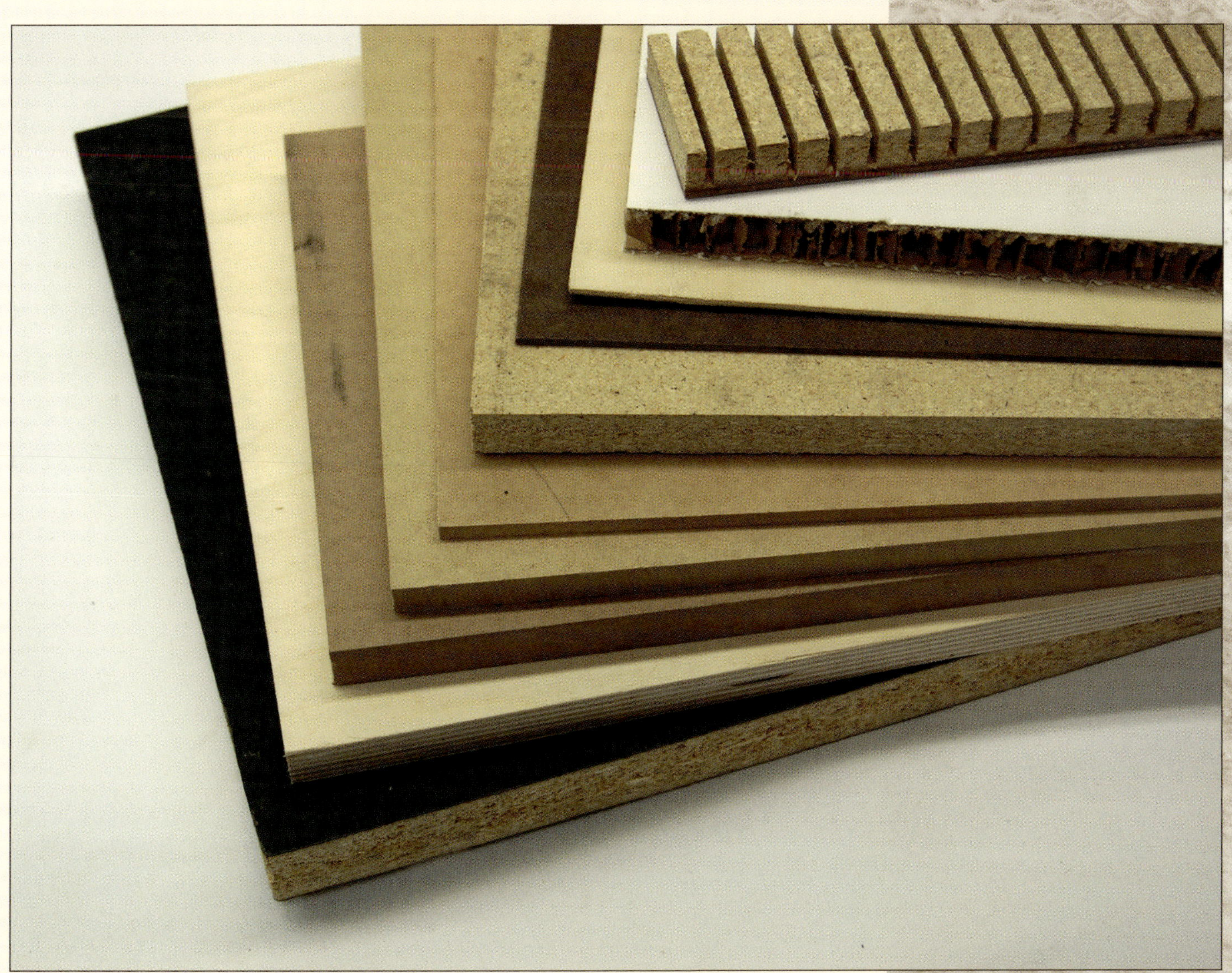

Various cores from top to bottom: kerfkore® - flexboard®, honey comb core (paper), .125" poplar ply, .125" masonite™, .75" particle board (flake board), ¼" MDF (medium density fiberboard), ½" MDF, .75" Medex®, (exterior MDF), 19mm Baltic birch plywood, 1.25" particle board with phenalic backer (balancer)

The Glue

There are a variety of glues available and choosing which one to use depends on the panel's application or function. Each glue has specific properties that can affect each application. Some of the properties and considerations to understand are:

- Flexural strength: This determines the rigidity of the glue line and directly affects the rigidity of the panel when it's dry.
- "Creep" or the movement of the veneer over the core after gluing.
- Sand-ability of bleed-through or glue glaze.
- Viscosity: How easily it flows and more importantly, how it soaks in and bleeds through the veneer.
- Open time: The working time before it tacks up. This is basically the amount of time you have to get the panel in the press. After the glue tacks, it can no longer bond to the veneer.
- Initial cure time: The amount of time it takes for the glue to "hold" (so a piece can be removed from a clamp or press), but has not yet reached its full structural properties.
- Cure time: Amount of time it takes to completely "set up" or cure and reach its full structural properties.
- Color: Using colored glue (pigmented closer the shade of the wood) will help hide any visible glue lines.
- Shelf life: This is more of an economical issue, as it depends on how much glue you use and how much you want to throw away. Read the labels for this time frame and when in doubt, test older glue.
- Toxicity: Again this does not directly affect the final panel performance, although typically the more toxic something is, the "better" the performance. Keep this in mind for personal safety and environmental considerations.

TWO CATEGORIES OF GLUE: chemical reaction/cross link versus evaporation. Chemical cross link glues, such as epoxy or urea formaldehyde, are stronger and resistant to water, but are also toxic. Evaporation glues are water-based, more flexible, and often reversible, which allows for easier repairs.

Understanding a specific type of glue's performance and how it affects a panel is critical in choosing glue. Upgrading the glue is not always the best solution.

For example: When veneering a thin 1/8" *flat panel* that will be used for a curved lamination later, a flexible PVA glue is a better choice than a rigid urea type. The rigid urea can be too strong, prevent easy bending and will possibly crack the panel during the bending process.

Or, when restoring an antique piece, the work should be performed "in kind" (often hide glue), meaning, stay true to the original method. Hide glue offers a reversible process.

I generally follow a few simple rules to help me select glue: they depend on the function and application of the final veneer panel. If I answer "yes" to any of the following questions, then I use a higher performance glue.

- Am I using a highly stressed grain, such as a burl, crotch, or multiple species with varying grain direction, with a likeliness to creep?
- Will the surface be exposed to moisture?
- Is the veneer oily?
- Is there an additional structure required such as a curved lamination or long spanning panel?
- What is the historical significance? If answered yes to this question, use hide glue as stated above.

My standard collection of glue supplies (from left to right): heating blanket for accelerating resin glues; digital scale for accurate glue measurements; various measuring cups (I like metric – milliliter divisions for easy math calculations); urea formaldehyde glue; Unibond 800™ resin and powder; West System ™ Epoxy resin and hardener liquid; Roo Glue™, a vinyl adhesive; Pro-set resin and hardener, thixotropic (thickened) epoxy; Titebond II™;Devon™ 5-minute epoxy; Weldwood ™ contact cement; Pro-glue™; urea formaldehyde powder glue (mixes with water); Loctite™ and hot shot™ CA (super) glue; Fastcap™ activator to accelerate CA glue; Krazy (CA) glue in small tubes; Heat Lock modified PVA for heat setting with an iron; Gorilla glue; polyurethane; Elmers® white PVA glue; Elmers® yellow PVA glue; Bloxygen argon gas to replace oxygen in half-empty glue containers to help prevent glues from reacting to moisture laden air or drying out; glue syringes; hide glue.

Below is a list of glue types, pro and cons, and my recommendations for application:

PVA (polyvinyl acetate) glue, typically known as white or yellow glue
Brand names: Elmer's® Titebond®, Betterbond™

Pros: easy clean up, inexpensive, can be heat set, remains flexible for post bending, quick set up time (typically one hour), non-toxic, left over glue can be reused, can be thinned (5% water) or thickened (with wood flour or corn starch).

Cons: non-gap filling, allows creep, short open time (2-5 minutes), one-year shelf life.

Note: There are many varieties and hybrid formulations with various additives that give them special qualities such as pigments to help conceal glue lines; thickeners to help prevent bleed through and glue glaze; extenders to give a longer open time, and "tacktifiers" (okay, I made that word up) to make the PVA glue perform somewhat like a contact adhesive but cure like a true PVA.

I prefer white glue over yellow. White has a longer open time and spreads more evenly. I use yellow (type II) only for small repairs when I want to heat set it with an iron.

Urea formaldehyde resin (plastic resin glue), two types: powder mixed with water and powder mixed with liquid resin
Brand names: Unibond 800, Plastic resin

Pros: long open time, rigid cure, prevents creep, sands easily, gap filling, long shelf life (resin powder type) if container is unopened, water resistant.

Cons: requires measuring and mixing (15% proportional window of variation), long cure time (heat sensitive – a heating blanket will speed up cure), messy, toxic, expensive and wasteful (mixed glue cannot be stored or reused).

Note: The powder/water type of urea formaldehyde resin has a six-month shelf life as the moisture in the air will slowly activate the glue. Keep the container tightly closed and stored in a cool dry place; a refrigerator works really well for prolonging the life.

These powder/water types are less expensive to ship due to weight and hazardous material charges than the resin version. Mixing is difficult, but lukewarm water helps: add a little at a time as you mix. This version also spreads poorly and has a tendency to bead up while spreading.

Powder/liquid resin types mix easier than powder/water versions, and spread more smoothly. A mixing paddle in a cordless drill helps mix both versions.

I use this glue for high quality jobs and any time my qualification list requires it. It is strong, ridged and resists creep and moisture. It is best for bent laminations.

Hide Glue: (traditionally used in hammer veneering and made from animal hides)

Brand names: Behlen's™, J.E. Moser's®

Pros: reversible (the glue can be reactivated and released with heat), durable (it has been used for centuries), great for piece-meal applications and seaming directly on the core.

Cons: susceptible to water, slow process, can not be used in a press, messy and stinky, requires double-boiler heated glue pot.

Note: This type of glue is great for high quality antique repairs, piece-meal and compound curved applications.

Epoxy

Brand names: West System®, Mas Expoxies, System Three®

Pros: waterproof, rigid, long open time, gap filling

Cons: requires measuring and mixing, long cure time (heat sensitive), messy, toxic, most expensive of glues and wasteful because once mixed, it can't be stored or reused.

Note: Epoxies can be purchased with a variety of properties to suit an array of specific applications such as gluing to metal or plastic. They are the waterproof and will adhere to almost everything.

Polyurethane

Brand name: Gorilla Glue

Pros: sticks to just about everything including fingers, clothes, hair; waterproof.

Cons: messy, expensive, thick and difficult to spread, expands during curing, short shelf life (cures from moisture in the air), shorter if container is opened and exposed to moisture-laden air.

Note: I rarely, rarely use this for veneer, although it's good for small projects and gluing to foam (requires the surface to be moistened with water to ensure a complete cure). It also requires firm pressing as the glue expands during curing.

Contact Adhesive (flammable or non-flammable)

Brand name: Hybond™, Weldwood™

Pros: quick turn around time, easy to find, no press required, great for stable material such as plastic laminate or fabric. It can also be used for paper-backed veneers.

Cons: *too flexible for raw veneer*, flammable types are toxic and stinky.

Note: These adhesives are not acceptable to use with raw veneer as they are too flexible. The veneer will eventually creep, lift or bubble. A solvent finish can also release the adhesive. They are only good for paper or phenolic backed veneers. *I do not use contact adhesive for any veneering job.*

The Press

There are a number of ways to press veneer: using a traditional screw press; a homemade fire hose pneumatic press; commercial-grade hydraulic monsters; vacuum bag systems; or a simple set of clamps. (And using sand bags or parking a car on a veneered board doesn't count—or work—I've tried them both!)

Whichever way you press, the most important concept is to apply even pressure (this is one reason why parking a car on your pile doesn't work).

Below are a variety of presses commonly used by professionals and hobbyists alike.

A massive screw press at Wendell Castle Studio. These are slow to use, but create an enormous amount of pressure. Crisscrossing the maple 4x4 cauls help to distribute the pressure.

A production hydraulic press at North Creek Woodworking. These often have heated platens, gauges, and adjustable pressure and can turn panels around within a few minutes when using the right glue. Large glue spreaders are frequently used in tandem for faster and more consistent glue application to the core. See background.

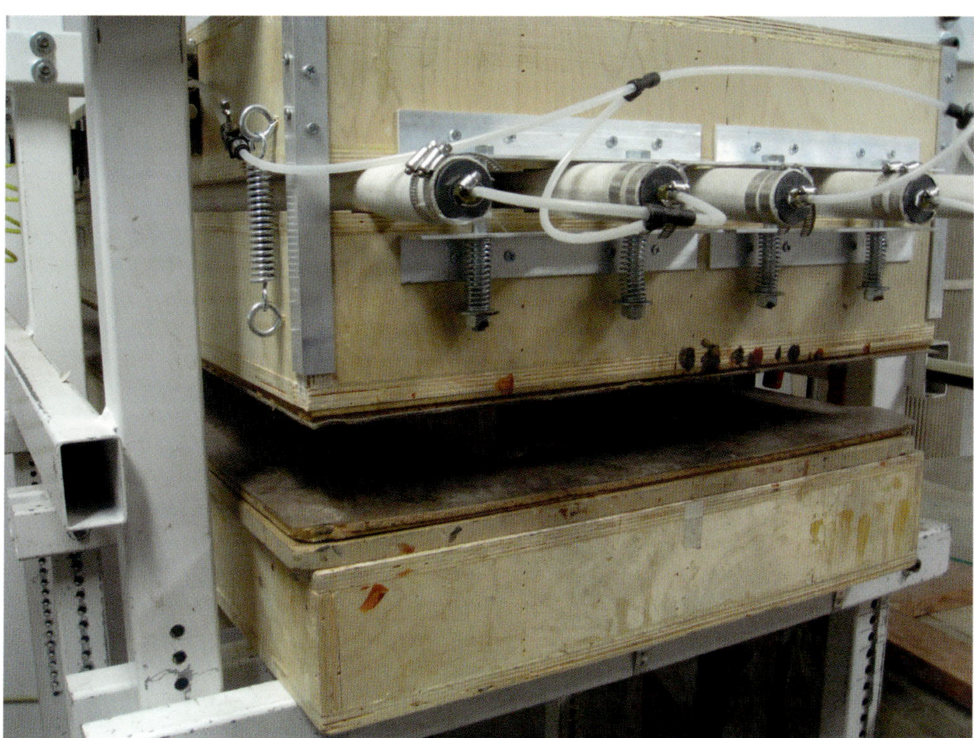

A homemade pneumatic press that uses fire hoses to move the platen (photo courtesy Andrew Muggleton).

Vacuum Presses

With the recent popularity of vacuum systems, this is the way to go for small shops. They are affordable, easy to use, and don't take up much floor space as the bag or frame can be easily stored away.

A vacuum frame press (photo courtesy Vacupress). This system is great for very quick processing. Large frames, as shown, or smaller portable ones (without a hinged bed) work very well for small panels. They require little set up time and store away easily.

From left to right: Hi-Flo industrial, .75 HP - 10 cfm oil-less electric rotary vane pump; Standard .33 HP - 6 cfm oil-less electric rotary vane pump; 6 cfm air-powered venture pump with automatic regulator.

The vacuum concept is simple: by using atmospheric pressure (which is 15 pounds per square inch at sea level), and by sucking most of the air out of a sealed void (a bag or frame) with the veneer lay-up inside, even pressure is applied and veneer is pressed onto the substrate.

Even pressure is the most important concern when pressing, not the amount of pressure; a vacuum inherently applies even pressure.

A vacuum is usually measured in terms of inches of mercury (Hg), similar to a barometer reading. There is no such thing as an absolute vacuum of 30″ Hg, much like there is no such thing as absolute zero, -459° F. The maximum vacuum one can pull is 29.9199", using a scientific vacuum pump, but most industrial vacuum pumps will pull 25"-27" Hg. Elevation affects the maximum amount of vacuum that can be achieved: subtract one inch for every 1000 feet above sea level.

Don't be fooled by the sound of it: these systems can generate plenty of pressure to do the job. To calculate the PSI (pounds per square inch) of a vacuum bag, simply divide the vacuum gauge (read in inches) by 2.

For example, 26 inches of vacuum will generate 13 PSI or 1872 lbs of pressure per square foot (13" Hg x 144" per SF). Most importantly, the pressure will be even. Note: The size of the bag does not effect this calculation.

Vacuum pumps are either electric or air powered.

Air powered pumps work with compressed air (via an air compressor) moving through a venturi that creates a vacuum. They can be either single- or multi-stage systems.

Electric pumps can be oil-lubricated, reciprocating or rocking piston, oil-less diaphragm, rotary vane or screw, or lobed rotor pump, all ranging in price and efficiency. I have a rotary vane pump.

Electrical pumps are graded either Scientific or Industrial. Don't bother with scientific pumps which can get close to 29.9" Hg. They are very expensive, slow, and, in fact, glue boils at 29" of vacuum.

Each system (electrical or air powered) can be either manual or automatic. Automatic systems turn the pump on when the vacuum falls to a selected setting such as 20" Hg and turn off when it reaches another selected setting such as 27" Hg.

Automatic systems are the way to go. I've never seen a vacuum system that didn't leak slightly, so to have a pump that automatically compensates for this is a must.

My first pump was an old cow milking pump that had to be left on as it chugged along. This got me very nervous when I had to leave the shop. A timer helped, but I still lost some sleep when I pressed overnight.

I still use my timer (shown in the photo) on my automatic pump, because with older units, sometimes the automatic switch can stick "on" and a timer can act as a redundant back up shut-off switch.

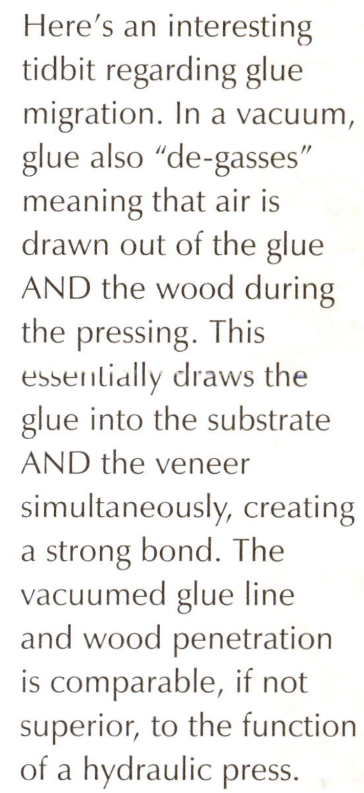
Here's an interesting tidbit regarding glue migration. In a vacuum, glue also "de-gasses" meaning that air is drawn out of the glue AND the wood during the pressing. This essentially draws the glue into the substrate AND the veneer simultaneously, creating a strong bond. The vacuumed glue line and wood penetration is comparable, if not superior, to the function of a hydraulic press.

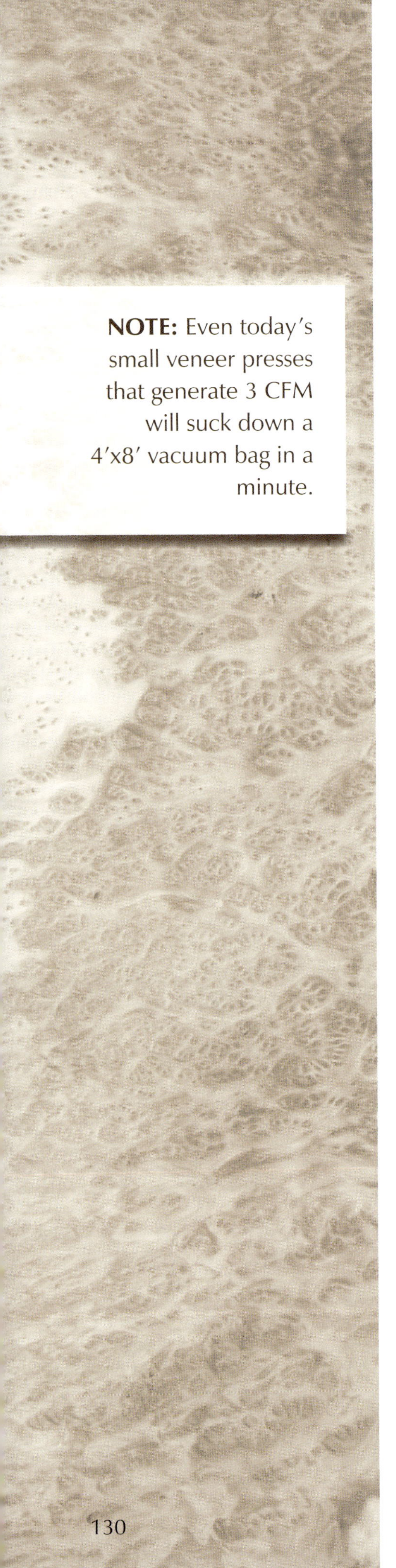

NOTE: Even today's small veneer presses that generate 3 CFM will suck down a 4'x8' vacuum bag in a minute.

The efficiency of a press is determined by two factors: vacuum level and flow.

The vacuum level is how *many* inches it can pull: 15" Hg is the minimum for flat veneer pressing, although I prefer to have at least 20" Hg. I typically press at 25"-27" Hg.

Vacuum flow is the *volume* or amount of air that can be moved in a relative amount of time measured in cubic feet per minute (CFM). The CFM *does* change depending on what level of vacuum is being pulled. For example, at 0" Hg the flow is the greatest. The greater the vacuum created, the less air there is, the less air that can be moved and the lower the CFM.

CFM will also determine how fast a large bag can be drawn down. If it is too slow, the glue might start to tack and set up. To avoid this on very low CFM pumps (less than 1 CFM), a holding tank, much like a compressor tank, can store a volume of vacuum that can be used to quickly evacuate a large bag.

The Bag

A vacuum press can be either a true bag or a frame with a single layer of plastic mounted to a frame.

In a true vacuum bag, the veneer panel goes inside the bag along with a platen (see page 131) and a vacuum is drawn applying equal pressure to all sides of the bag. A vacuum bag is great for curved laminations and is often used for helix spiral staircase stringers. This bag system applies equal pressure to both sides of a lamination.

A vacuum frame system has one layer of plastic attached to a frame with a gasket on the bottom side of the frame. The frame is simply placed over the veneer panel and onto a smooth non-porous surface. The bottom gasket makes a seal and allows for a vacuum to be drawn.

"Bag" material is typically either vinyl or polyurethane that ranges in thickness, size, and price. Polyurethane bags are more durable, flexible, and expensive. They also have more stretch and will conform around curved shapes more easily.

On a tight budget, any large heavy-duty plastic bag will work. A furniture store often has large bags that are used for beds and couches, but these will easily tear and are not good for more than one use.

Both of these systems requires a method that allows the air to be completely evacuated. These methods can be an aeration or "breather" blanket or a grooved platen. These prevent the bag from sealing itself off and stopping the vacuum flow.

Bags come in a variety of sizes and can be custom made. They are either polyurethane or vinyl and typically two thicknesses: 20 and 30 mil. My everyday bag is 30 mil polyurethane and takes a 4′ x 8′ sheet.

A grooved platen is commonly used in either system (bag or frame). The grooves act as passageways for the air to be completely removed during vacuuming. The photo shows the vacuum port intersecting with one of the grooves.

In lieu of grooves, a breather fabric can be placed over the veneer panel and vacuum port to allows a path for air to be drawn out. A bleeder fabric is a coarse polyethylene mesh. Window screening will not work as it is too dense.

Application Of The Glue: The Glue Up

Applying the glue can be done using a variety of methods. The most important issue is to apply it evenly; the second most important issue is using the correct amount of glue.

Each glue, substrate, and wood species requires a different amount of glue.

Most failures are due to too much glue, not enough glue, uneven application, glue drying (glazing over) before pressing (typical with PVA glues) and/or glue not curing (as with urea glues) due to cold temperatures or poor mixing.

The right amount of glue is approximately 12-24 grams per square foot. These are very general numbers, as absorption rates change considerably depending on the species of wood and type of substrate.

To confirm this and gain a feel for the right amount of glue to use, simply spread glue on a 12″ square core and weigh it before and after the glue is applied. This will give you a general starting point for how much glue is required for each type of glue and material you're using.

This calculation is very helpful in determining how much resin glue to mix up per job (as the more expensive glues such as urea and epoxy glues can't be re-used).

I keep a glue-up book for future reference and record the amount of glue I use on how many square feet of each application for each project. This really helps on larger projects.

Notched trowels (no larger than 1/16″ V groove), disposable roller and a hopper roller are all good applicators. A re-sealable bin prevents a PVA glue roller from drying out, is good for quick use and you can avoid cleaning the roller after every use.

I like to use a hopper roller applicator for PVA glue. It applies the glue evenly and allows you to pull the red level back and use the roller only (without adding more glue) to evenly spread the applied glue.

NOTE: to store a roller applicator for multiple uses during the day, keep it in a sealed bucket with an inch of water in the bottom to create a humid environment so the glue roller won't dry and glaze over.

When using urea plastic resin glue or epoxy, I use either a notched trowel or disposable foam paint roller. Cleaning these is impossible.

Before applying any glue, be sure both surfaces are clean of dust and/or small wood chips.

OVER SIZING the veneer and panel gives me plenty of room for error, when alignment isn't critical. If I need to pre-cut the core to its final size and align the veneer exactly, I adhere small alignment blocks with double-stick tape onto the veneer during a dry alignment test before gluing.

Roll the glue out evenly. I overlap the previous layer glue by 1/3 on each pass when I use my hopper roller.

Close the applicator by pulling the red lever back and roll perpendicular to the previous application direction. This smooths out all the glue evenly. Work quickly.

Carefully align the panel on top of the veneer. My veneer is typically 1″ oversized than my core, and my core is 1″ oversized from its final dimension.

Although you could have a number of different sized bottom cauls, I simply use one 4′ x 8′ caul for every press, even for small panels.

TIP: I cover the sharp corner of the veneer panels with 1/16″ sheet rubber to help protect the bag.
I also cover my glue caul with paper to keep it clean from glue squeeze out. The glue caul is 3/4″ MCP (melamine coated particle board) and does not have grooves in it. The caul must be smooth and clean. Mine is just slightly smaller than the vacuum platen, which is also 3/4″ MCP, and has grooves in it. I also round over the caul and platen edges to protect the bag.

Pressing Steps:

Here is a brief description of how I typically press a panel:

- I cut an oversized core, typically one inch over its final size.
- I cut the veneer face oversized by one inch over the core.
- I typically use either white PVA glue or urea formaldehyde glue, depending on the application.
- If I am using white PVA glue, I press the back first for one hour, then press the front for 3-6 hours.
- If I'm using urea formaldehyde glue, I press the back and front at the same time due to urea's longer open time. I use an additional top caul, oversized by one-half inch (more on this below).
- Even though the veneer is all securely taped together, I like to get it in the press as soon as possible, especially with a multiple piece panel (called a "sketch face"). The different veneer pieces will continue to expand and contract possibly warping the entire sketch face.
- After pressing, remove the tape the same day or keep the panel covered and away from light, until the tape is removed to prevent shadowing. (UV rays can bleach the exposed wood and not the wood under the tape).
- Trim the excess veneer with a router using a flush trim bit.
- If glue glaze is present, I lightly wash the veneer surface with lukewarm water and scrub the glaze off with a green ScotchBrite™ pad. I know what you're thinking—all that water! See Chapter 8.

I also use rails with rollers on them to make moving the panel in and out of the bags easier. These were salvaged from an old grocery conveyer track.

The end of the bag is sealed by wrapping the bag around a plastic rod and clipping another C channel rod over the inner rod. Use duct tape to seal any pin hole leaks in older bags.

11

Spiral Match

Once you step away from traditional linear seaming and symmetrical pattern matching, the design door opens wide. In keeping with my rebellious thinking and desire to have more artistic freedom when working with veneer, I developed the spiral match pattern.

To a certain extent, the spiral is still a symmetrical or predictable pattern, but it is a good starting point for my freeform method of seaming and pattern composition development. This method allows for any design the mind can imagine.

My personal goal in using this technique is to create a pattern that is right on the edge of appearing to be a natural creation. For me this provides a sense of curiosity when viewing the pattern: Is this natural? Where did you find this piece of wood? These are the type of questions I receive from first time viewers.

The following piece was designed for a landscape architect. As with most of my commissions, I was given functional requirements such as size, storage space needed and a general request of the color harmony, but the veneer composition was completely up to me. I decided to emulate a springtime fiddlehead fern, which was a perfect opportunity to show off my spiral match.

In an attempt to keep the process simple, first I explain the layout and then address precise alignment techniques of the sap/heartwood seam.

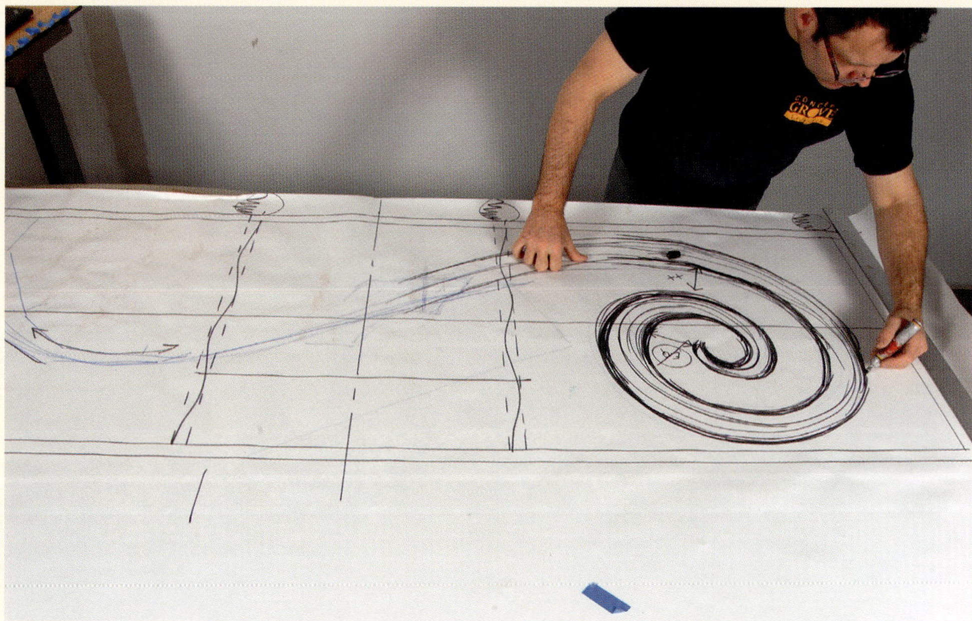

Sketch out the spiral in a full-scale drawing of the cabinet. The tapered stem (I refer to this as the sapwood field) represents a fiddlehead fern and will be expressed using contrasting sapwood within the burl.

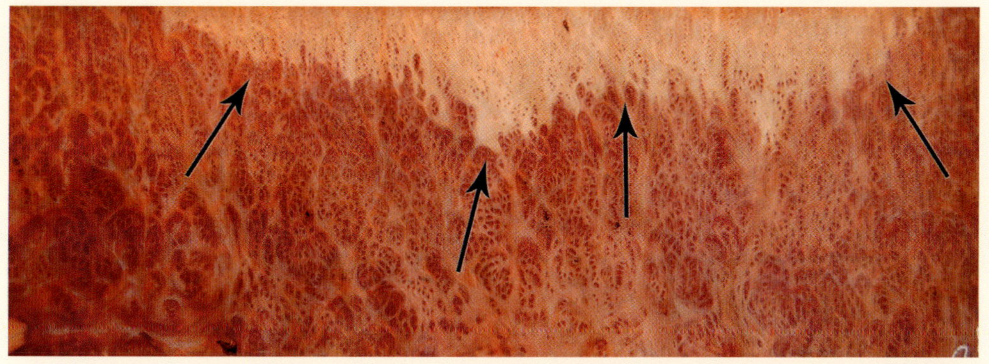

When purchasing the veneer, find a figure that contains both concave and convex curves as well as straight-ish areas. This is a great advantage and gives you the most flexibility to create any design.

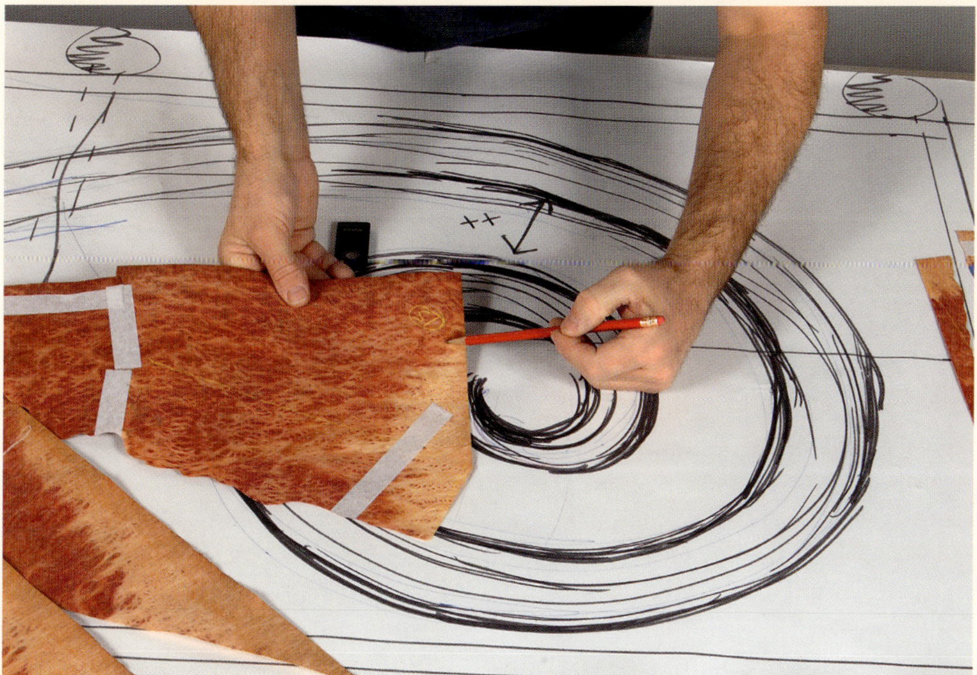

The fundamental challenge is to locate a section of veneer with a similar curve to the drawing between the sap and heartwood edge. I do this by eye, but for critical lines I use tracing paper to help align the curve. Here I've selected my beginning piece and have decided to work with the outside sap / heartwood edge first.

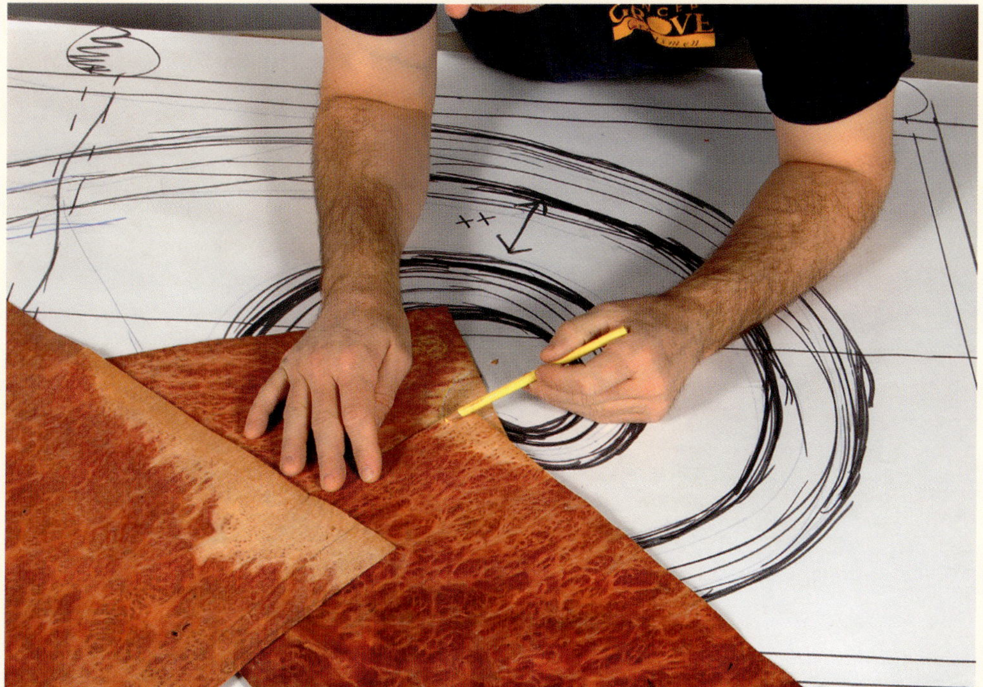

Working with a second piece of veneer with a similar curve I visually line the two sapwood edges up to "see" if the arc looks right. It is important to me that the transition between the two curves is graceful. I sketch directly on the veneer to help in this alignment. Be sure to leave enough overlap between the two sections (at least one inch) for cutting the wavy contour seam.

After taping the two pieces of veneer together (precise sapwood alignment will come later), draw the furthest boundary of the heartwood for removal.

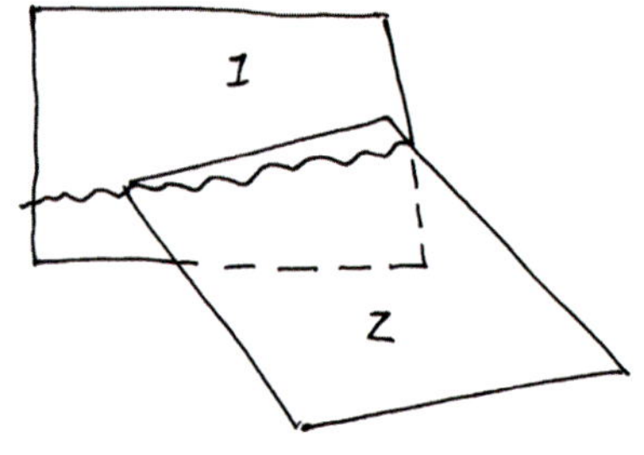

Cut out only the pieces that you need, which helps in handling and seaming.

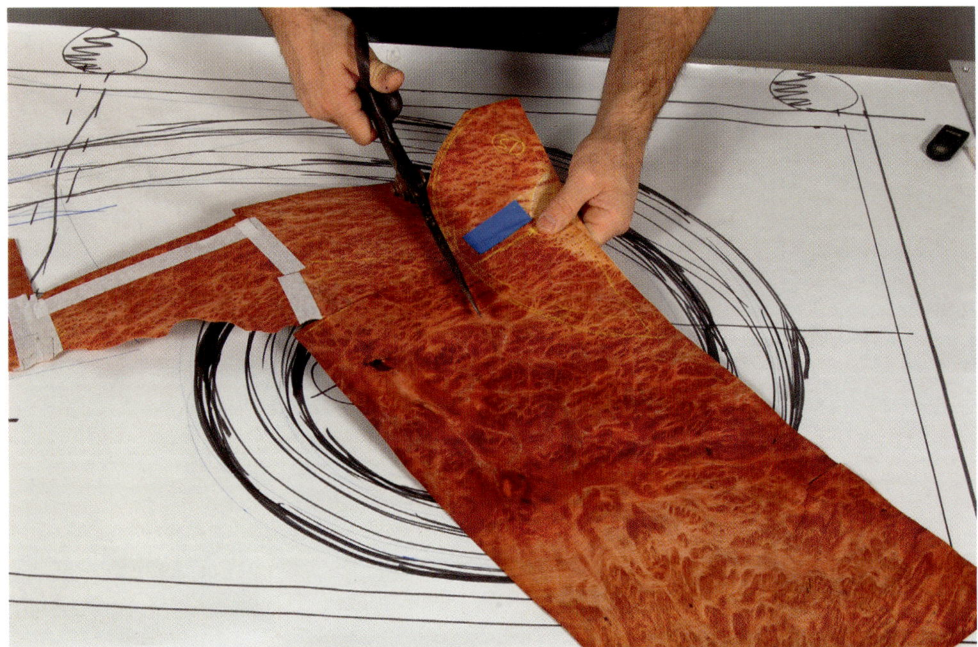

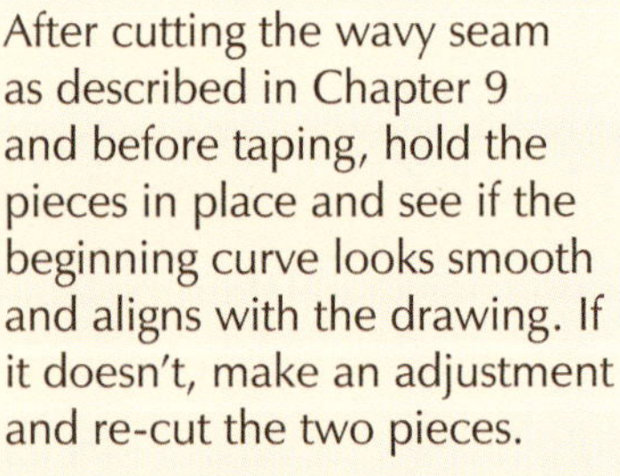

After cutting the wavy seam as described in Chapter 9 and before taping, hold the pieces in place and see if the beginning curve looks smooth and aligns with the drawing. If it doesn't, make an adjustment and re-cut the two pieces.

After taping the first two pieces together, repeat the previous step with the third piece of veneer. Again, select an accommodating curve, overlap, align and cut. I review various methods of aligning the sap/heartwood seam later in this chapter.

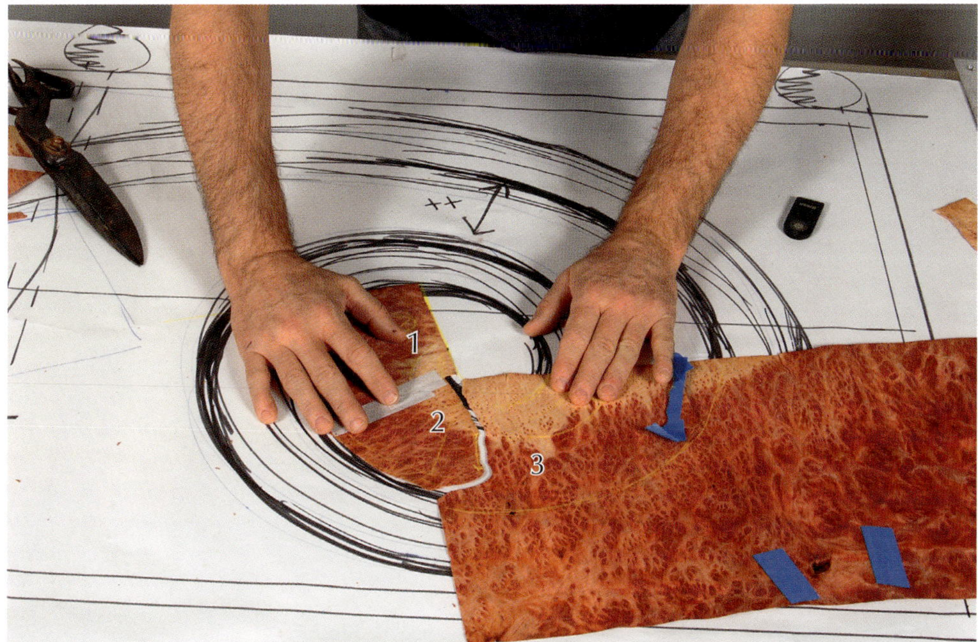

Check the alignment and curve again, and veneer tape it together.

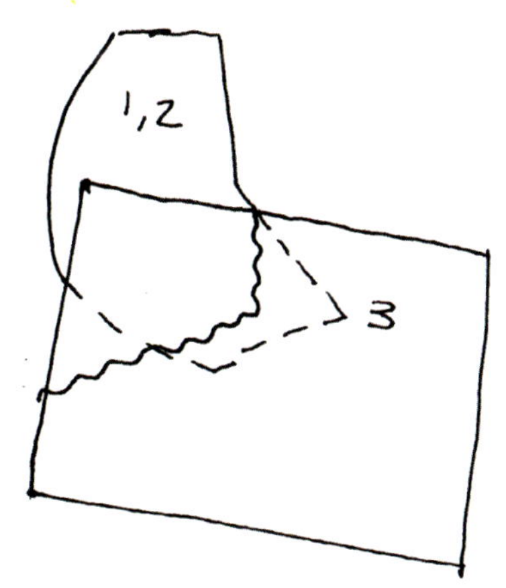

Flip over the pieces; take a look at the sap/heartwood edge alignment and the fluidity of the curve.

As I work around, I continue to roughly sketch the fiddle back fern's curve on each veneer section. Translating the original spiral to the veneer can be performed with tracing paper as in photo on page 24. I often wing it and visualize the original spiral and simply sketch as I go.

Visualize the curve between the next two pieces.

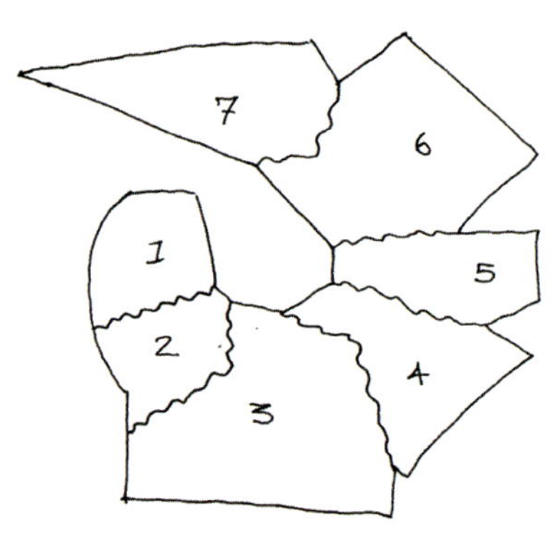

It is important to keep an eye on the amount of sapwood in the center field in the original drawing. Here I have wandered off from the field's center line (so much for winging it!). To solve this, I select an opposing piece with enough sapwood to make up the difference. No worries.

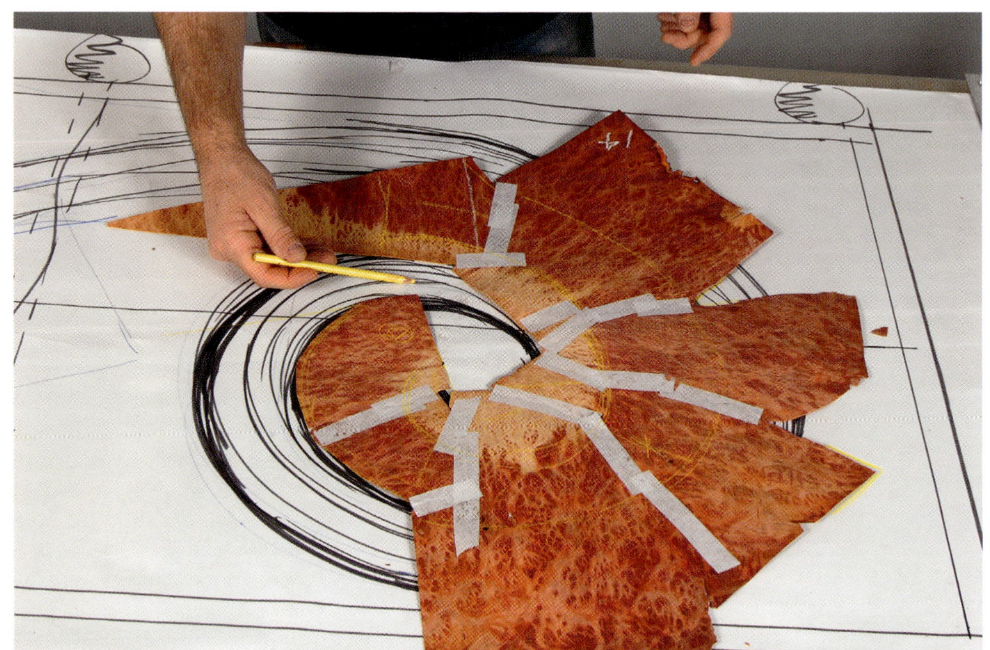

When I have enough of a smooth spiral to easily "see" its progression, I stop working the outside sapwood edge.

NOTE: If the grain and/or color vary too much from end to end, a slip match will reveal a contrasting seam. A book match will be your best choice (mirror matching both sides with the same color and grain) and of course using a wavy contour seam helps conceal this seam.

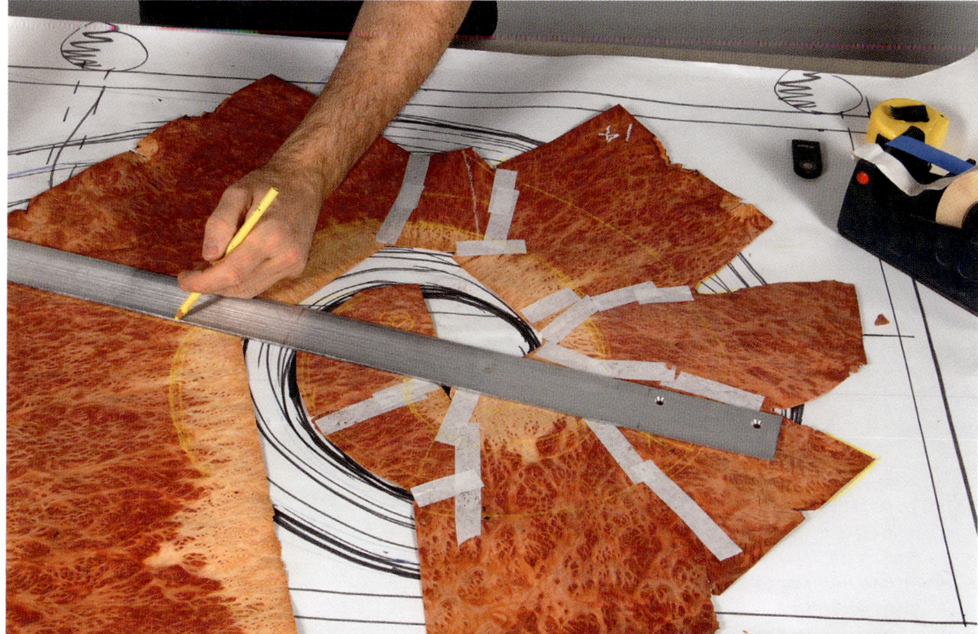

Whenever possible I like to cut the heartwood seam in a radial direction. Here I use a straightedge aligned with the center of the spiral to draw the general radial direction.

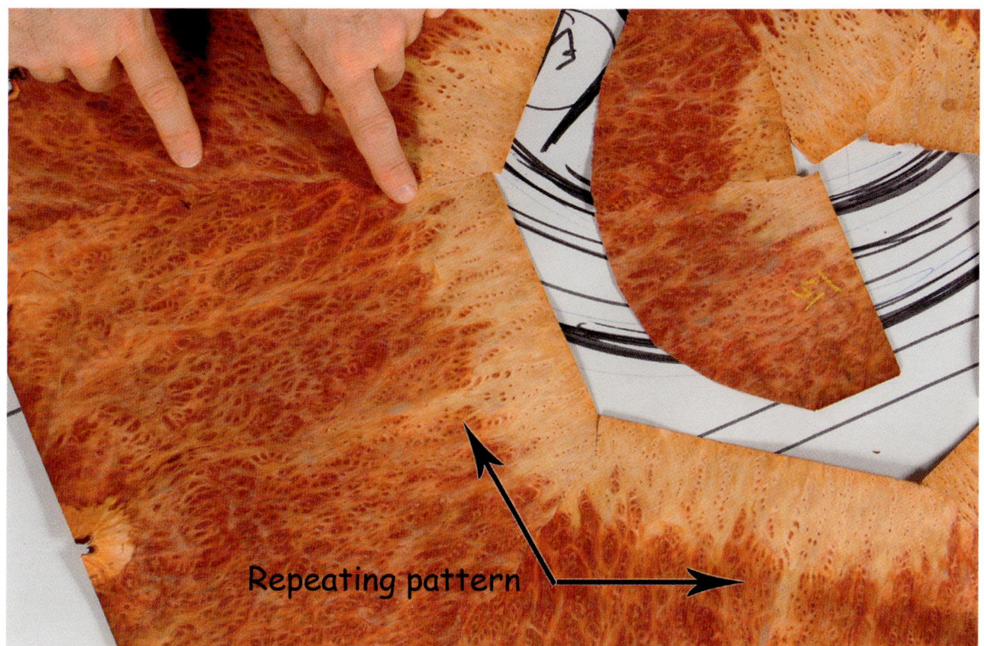

Constantly check the back side for sap/heartwood alignment and wavy contour seam for quality.

It is worth noting that as the number of pieces add up, a repeating grain pattern might start to show.

It can be challenging to locate and align the first opposing piece that defines the start of the spiral. Tracing paper helps this process.

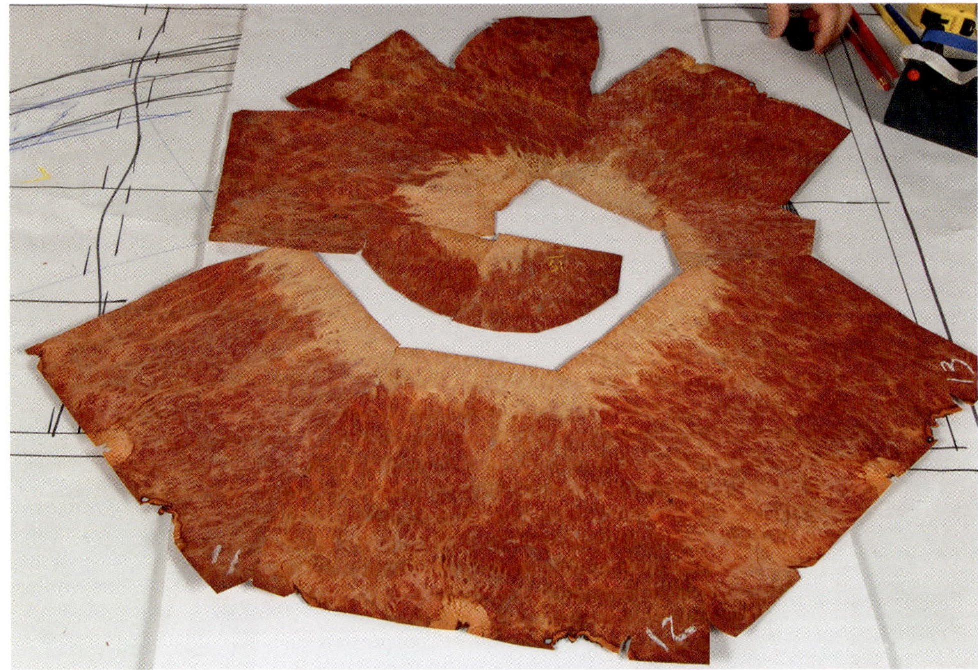

Check the back for an overall smooth curve and sap/heartwood seam alignment. Now it is time to seam the inside side of the sap/heartwood match.

To ensure proper alignment with the original drawing and assist on the inside curve layout, sketch out the interior edge perimeter of the veneer onto a large sheet of tracing paper (shown in blue).

Also sketch out the outside sap/heartwood seam (shown in red).

Align the tracing paper over the original sketch and tape it in place far outside of the working area (see blue tape on left). Trace the original spiral (shown in black).

Move various samples around under the tracing paper until the alignment and curve look right. Keep in mind that there is always room for changing the original drawing slightly.

Slide and align the taped sketch face under the tracing paper and tape it to the work surface. Slip the first new opposing inside sap/heartwood section between the tracing paper and the taped outside sketch face to form the spiral tip. Align the new piece to the traced spiral and tape to the sketch face. This registers the two inside and outside curves to the original spiral drawn on the tracing paper. Confused yet? Hang in there!

The next step is to identify the cutting path. The sapwood center seam is not a critical alignment—just keep it in the middle of the sapwood field and be sure to stay in the overlapped areas.

There are a number of ways to transfer this line, such as using carbon paper, or sketching under the paper while looking through it from above, as shown. Here, I am simply reaching under the tracing paper and following the line through the paper.

Once aligned, hold firmly in place and tape the new leaf onto the spiraled leaves below. Here I adjust my original spiral sketch to better transition the beginning of the spiral tip with the veneer.

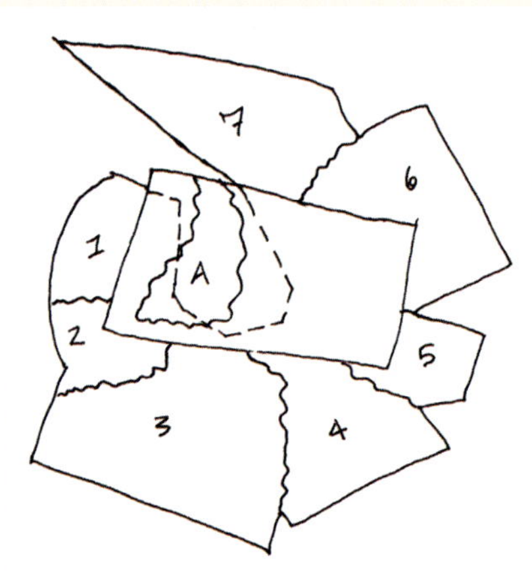

When looking through the tracing paper, sketch out the sapwood center seam onto the veneer below (shown in yellow on the tracing paper).

It is important to keep track of the enter and exit cutting paths to yield the most remaining material. This will give you room for overlapping the following pieces. Above, the piece is cut and ready for taping. Think of these as pie pieces.

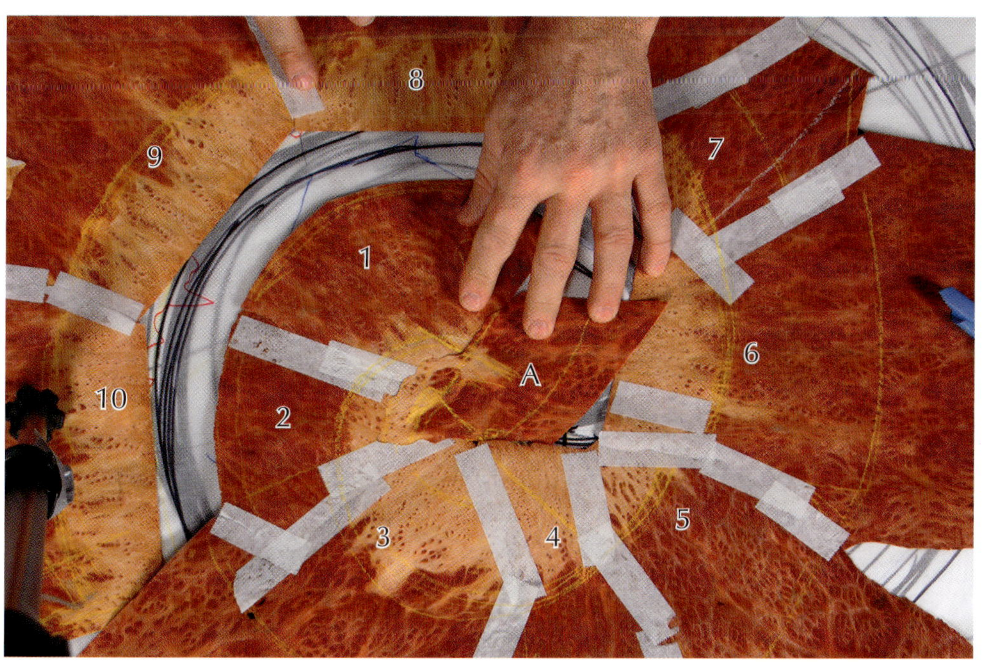

The spiral tip typically is the hardest element to align. The sapwood field width also sets the tone for the rest of the spiral. I like to start with a narrow portion and gradually widen this field.

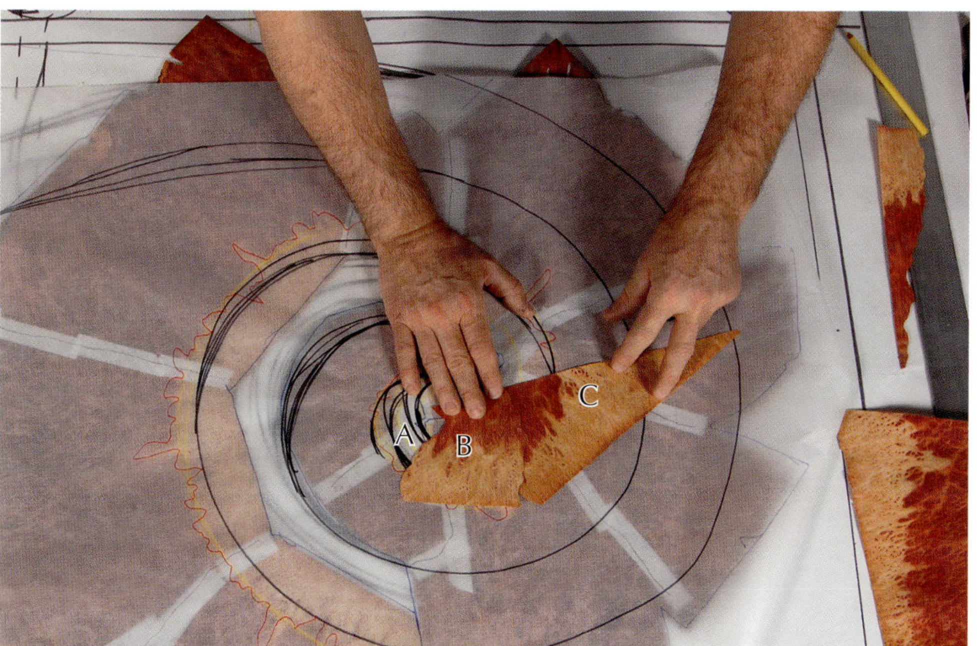

The spiral can be created piece by piece or in sections. Here I've put two pieces together that follow the curve, then added them to the previous piece in a similar manner, aligning and tracing through the paper.

Carefully draw the cutting paths to ensure that the cut will go through both overlapped pieces.

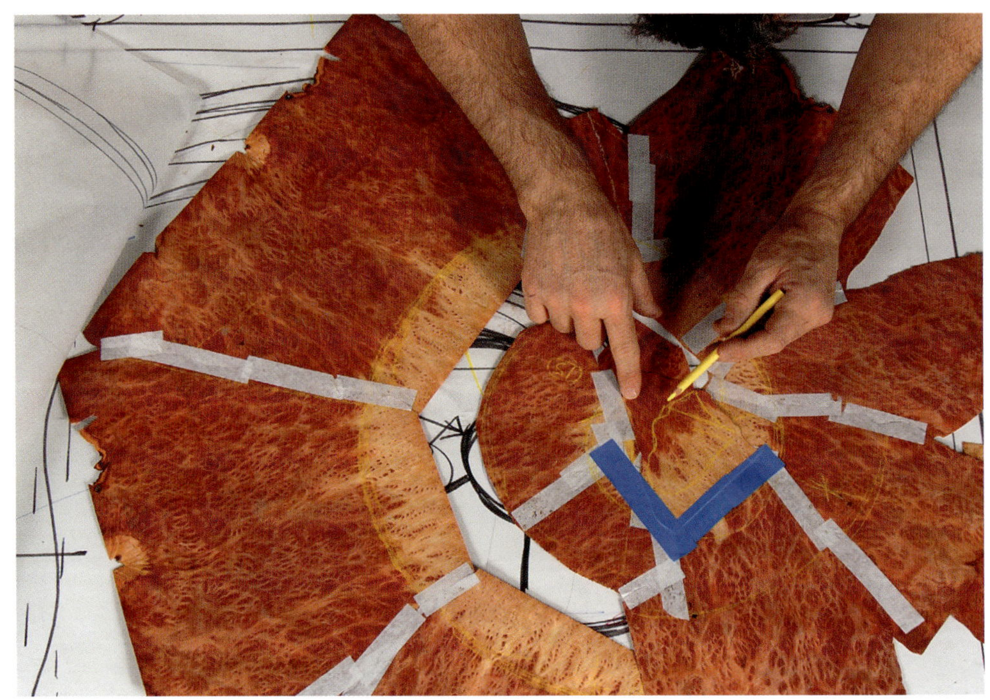

Aligning

Beside a smooth curve, the sapwood/heartwood alignment is most critical. I locate this critical intersecting spot on the lower piece by looking through the veneer tape and marking it with an "X" (this is a good reason for using white tape).

Hitting this single alignment spot is *very critical*, and there are a few methods you can use. The majority of the cutting path is not critical as long as you stay on an overlapped section.

One alignment method is using the tracing paper to precisely transfer this spot to the next top piece. See bottom photo on page 150. Once you register the top piece, tape it in place, and transfer the lines through the tracing paper.

A quicker method is to simply align this critical spot by eye. Hold the new veneer section firmly in place, peek under the edge of the leaf and align the point by eye. This works best if the alignment point is close to the edge. It does take practice but once you are proficient, it saves a lot of time.

Aligning the sap/heartwood seam is a *very critical* step to ensure that the final spiral looks "real," with smooth transitions from piece to piece. Here I peer under the veneer to visually align the two "X" points.

Once the two spots are aligned, hold the top veneer spot with a pencil (not shown in photo) and adjust the curve by slightly rotating the piece back and forth using your pencil as an axis point. I use dividers to confirm my width. I want the sapwood field to gradually get wider. In lieu of a pencil, I use a dentist's pick and literally pin the two leaves together while I rotate for alignment. See bottom photo on page 151. "T" pins also work well. See below for other locating options.

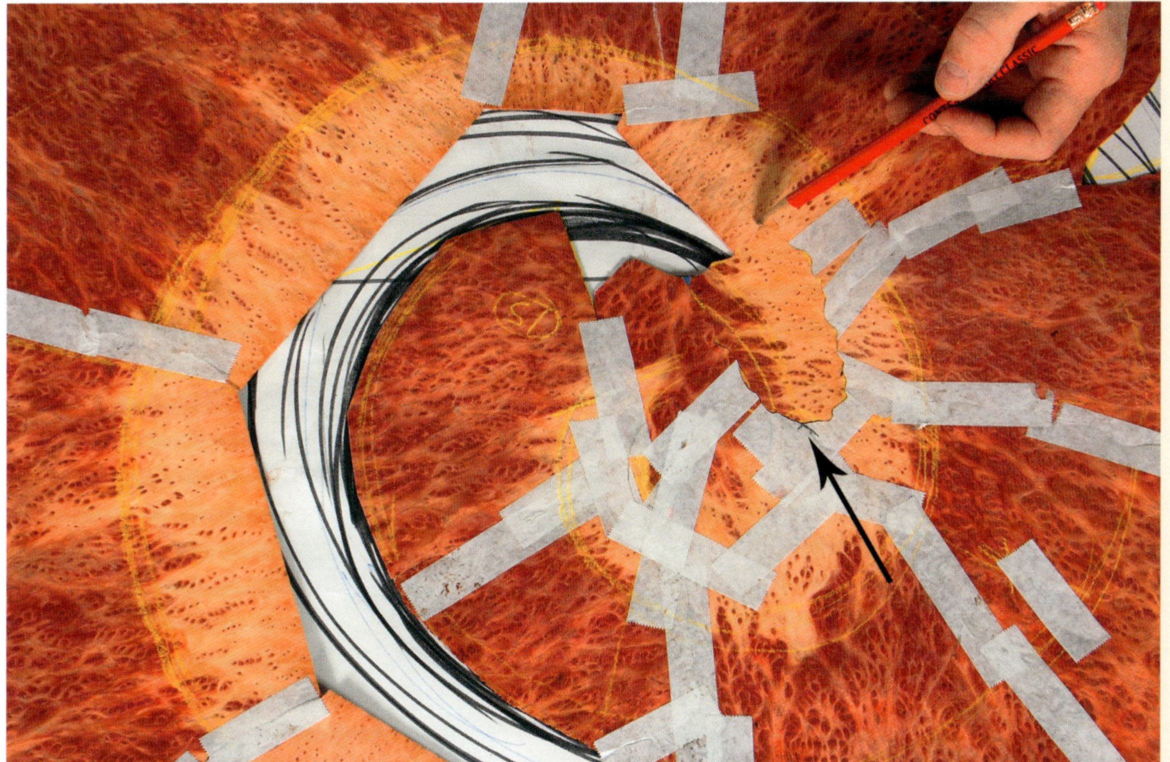

Here is the piece in place before taping. You can see half of the remaining critical intersecting "X" (bottom of patch) and the perfect wavy seam located with a pencil.

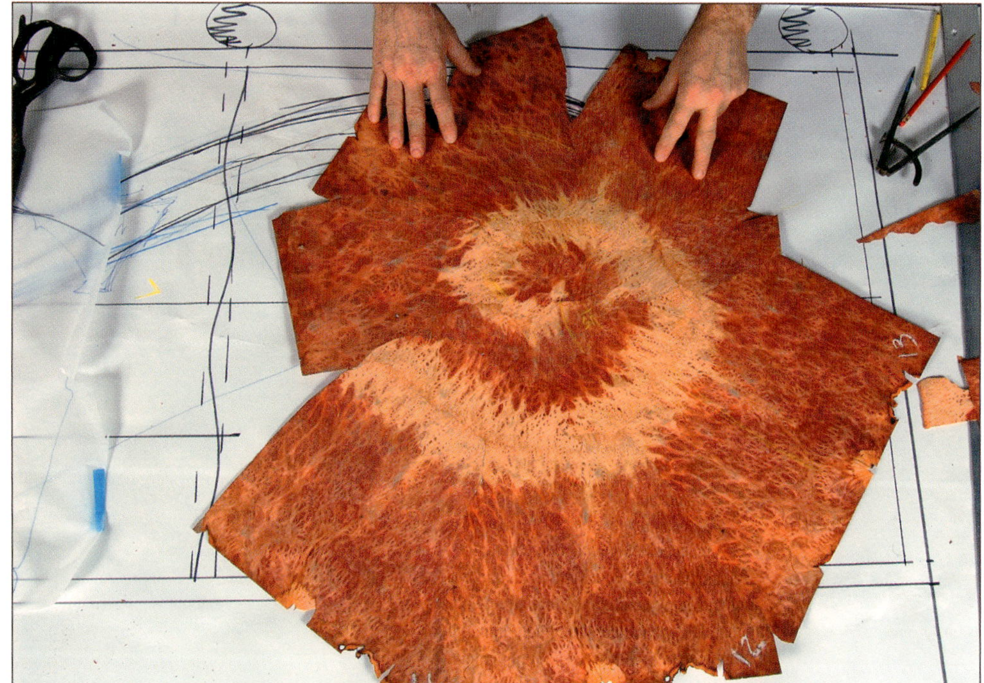

View of the spiral from the back after a number of inside pieces are cut in. Looking Good!

Another way to identify the sap/heartwood edge is to flip the sketch face over and trace a few inches of the grain from the back. This is especially helpful if your tape is getting a bit thick and you can't exactly see the spot you want to intersect.

Working from the top face, flip over the tracing paper, line up the grain and trace over the tape.

The exact connection point is now located on the veneer tape.

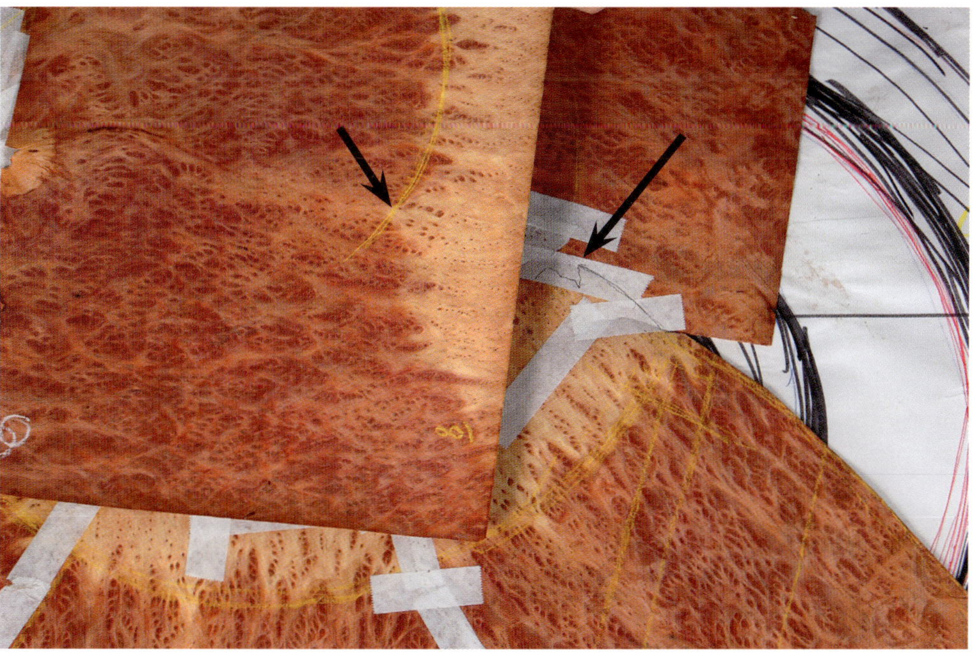

On the next piece, the curve line is sketched out and the intersection is located with an "X".

Place the dentist pick point over the connecting point on the lower layer of veneer and rest the back end of the dentist tool on the table.

Slightly raise the tip straight up while resting the back end on the table, and slide the upper veneer sheet under the tip. Align the new veneer point to the tip, then lower the tip and pierce through the top sheet, pinning the two sheets together exactly at the connection point.

This allows the upper sheet to be rotated easily so you can visually align the curve. I use this method most often as it is quick, very accurate and pins the two pieces together to ensure alignment while I adjust the curve.

Use a dentist's pick when the connection point is too far away from the edge to peek under or you don't wish to use tracing paper.

After securing the aligned top sheet in place with masking tape, peek under the veneer and draw your cutting path. Again, this seam is not critical, as long as the path stays in the overlapped heartwood fields. Tracing paper can also be used to locate this seam.

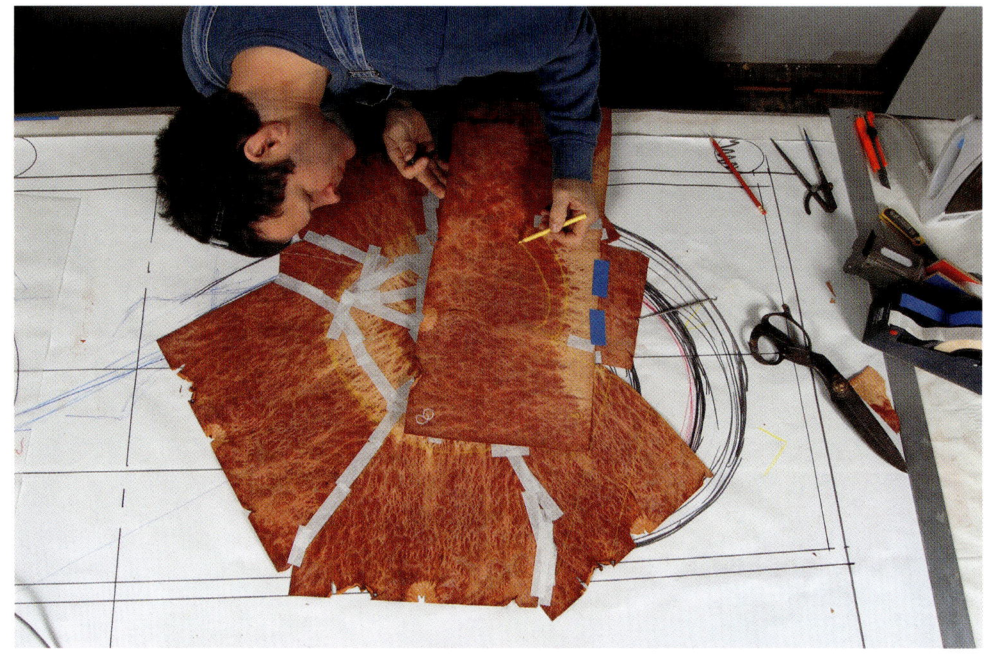

Testing the fit after cutting the double bevel wavy contour seam.

Viewed from the back, a wedge of heartwood will need to be spliced in. The method is the same as a repair as shown in Chapter 4, repair, page 50.

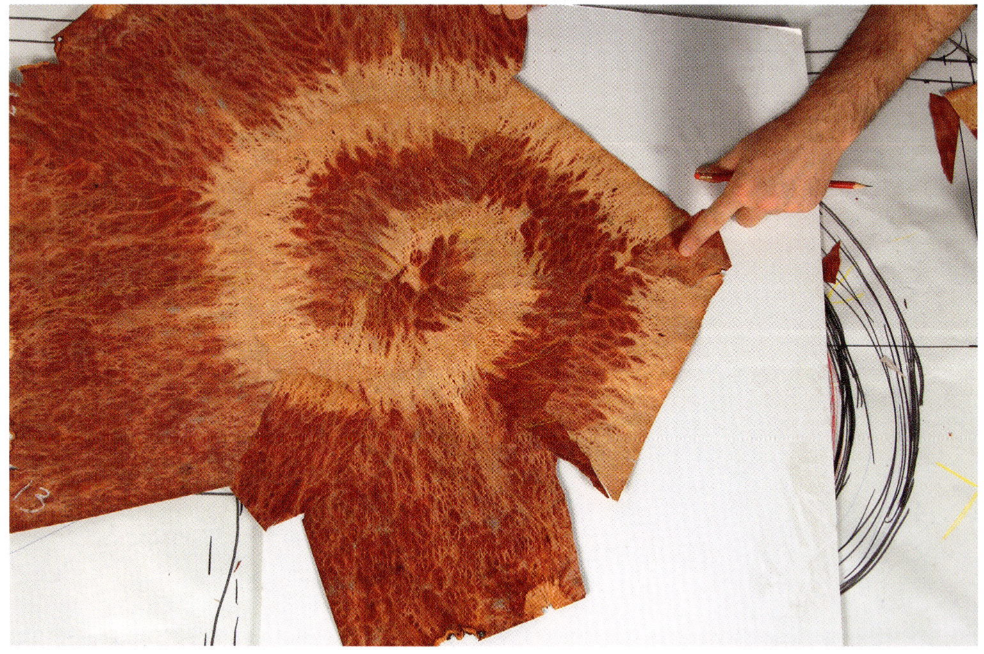

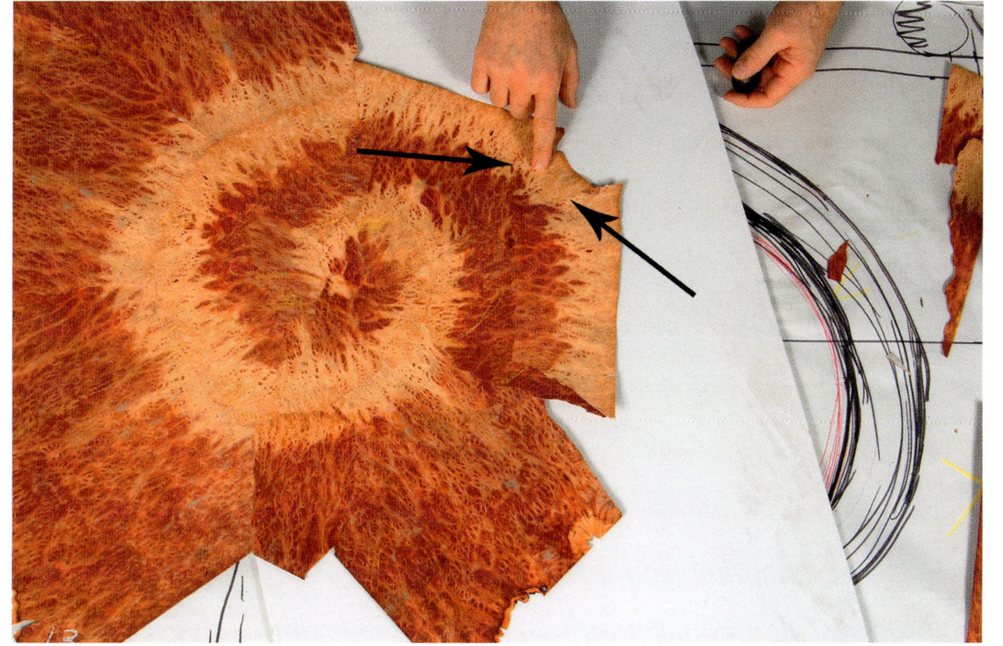

The repair after splicing in a piece of sapwood. Again, be sure to align both connecting sap/heartwood seams to ensure a clean transitional line.

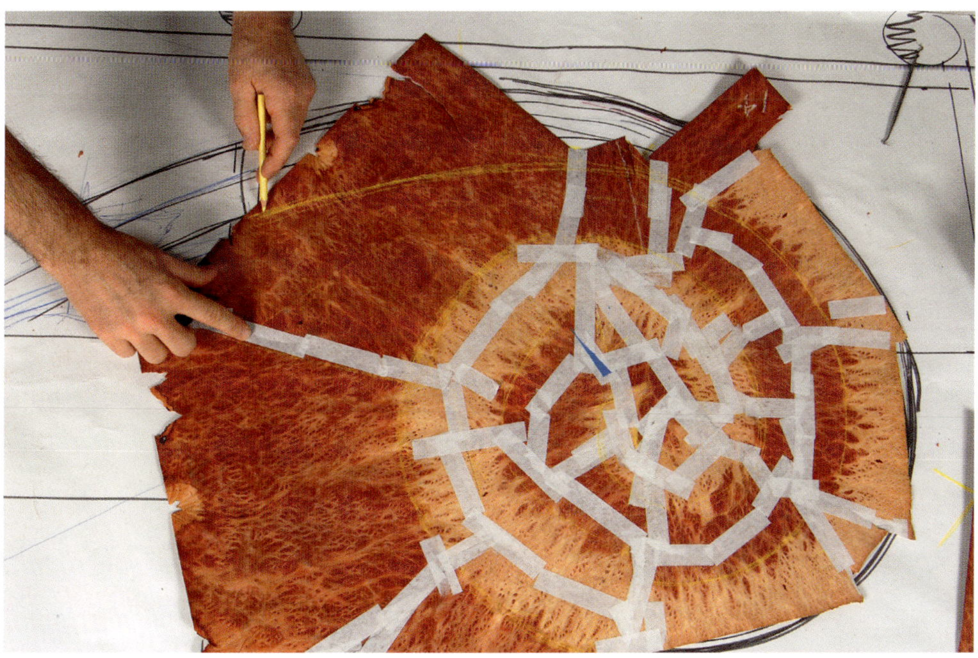

Sketching out the general line of the exiting curve.

As I start running out of material, identify pieces that have the correct curves and mark out the section length.

Measure the number of pieces along the curve to confirm that you have enough material. I've turned the spiral counterclockwise to reduce the number of pieces that I need. At this point I have abandoned the orientation of my original sketch.

As the sapwood field gets wider my overlap reduces considerably. This particular overlap seam will be barely a 1/8".

Because I am so close to the edge, I use blue masking tape to protect the cut from splitting.

In this wider sapwood field, I am careful to stay within the overlap areas. I again use tracing paper to help layout this center seam.

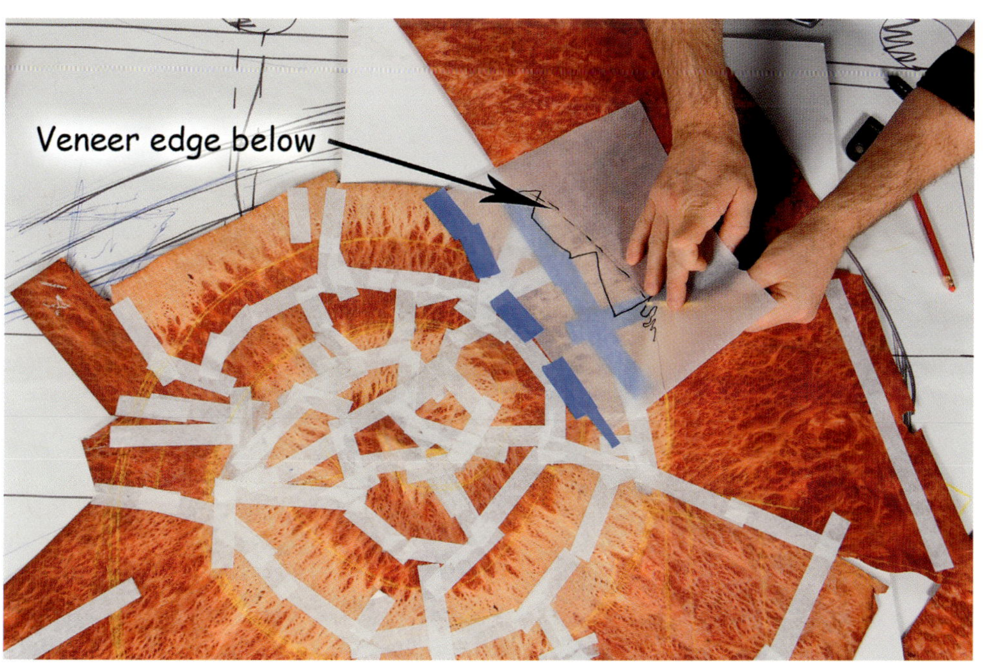

Transfer the edge to the next piece of veneer using a smaller piece of tracing paper that helps identify the cutting path.

Another method to help locate the alignment point is to literally see through the veneer by using a flashlight from underneath.

After the spiral is complete, assemble the left curved field in a similar manner. I use a 1/4″ dowel to help align the transitioning curves.

Select and locate the last two connecting sapwood pieces.

Trim off excess for easier handling and to use as patch matching material.

Seam together a heartwood field to fill in the remaining outer voids.

On larger double bevel cuts, I extend my table with a sheet of 1/4″ foam core for additional support.

With a foot-operated on/off control switch, I can easily start and stop the cut and move to the rear and continue pulling the work through the cut. Since this cut is greater than my 32″ scroll saw throat, I peel up the two cut halves to clear the throat. This method works on even shorter scroll saw throats.

I've added even more foam core to be sure the entire field is supported and easily slides along while I cut the two halves.

Back to the table for final veneer taping.

Voila! Final inspection.

Door Panel Alignment

Carefully mark the exact location to lay out and align the door panels to be pressed. I use calibrated spacers to establish the door seams. See next photo.

Transfer the sapwood field location onto the door to align the edge veneer. Calibrated horseshoe spacers are great for setting the door seam. The red spacers are exactly 1/8″ and the blue are 1/16″.

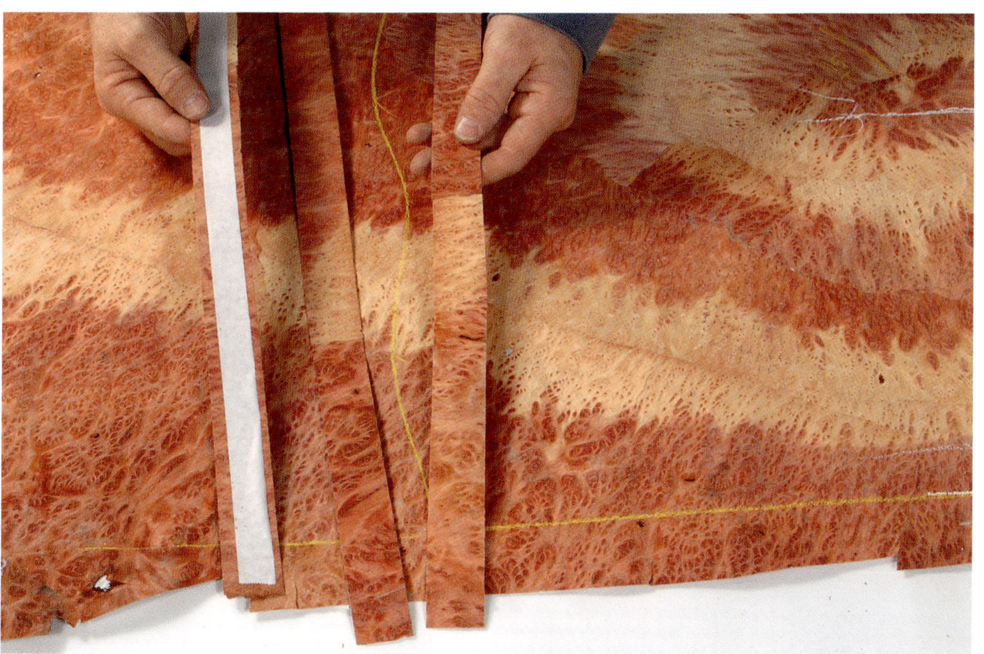

Cut and seam edging strips with sapwood field that match the width on the corresponding door face. The final appearance will look as if the door is solid, as the sapwood wraps around the door edge.

In keeping with my wave theme, my door seams are wavy too. Glue the interior edges together all at once using the opposing door edge as a clamping caul.

Glue the edging on both opposing sides at once using an 1/8″ strip of rubber to help compensate for any minor inconsistencies and to act as a glue barrier.

The final dresser includes a carved case with a copper polychrome finish.

Appendix A
Wood Facts
COURTESY OF DANZER GROUP

DID YOU KNOW...

... that no forest is destroyed to harvest wood used for decorative purposes?
... that only a few trees have the properties necessary for their wood to be used for decorative purposes?
... that for this reason only a very small portion of a timber harvest (1 5%) can be made into veneer and only slightly more into lumber?
... that ten percent of today´s forest areas would be enough to meet the worldwide demand for timber sustainably (including paper production)?
... that more than half of the wood harvested in the world is burned to generate energy?
... that the forested area in most industrial countries is growing, especially in the hardwood forests of North America and Europe, and that less timber is cut than grows back?
... that each tree absorbs an average of six kilograms of CO_2 from the atmosphere each day and thus makes a decisive contribution to protecting the climate?
... that every cubic meter of lumber has drawn a quarter of a metric ton of CO_2 out of the atmosphere?
... that managed forests, thanks to their high proportion of young, strong, growing trees, enable CO_2 to be extracted?
... that an old, unmanaged forest produces as much CO_2 through processes of decomposition and decay as it stores, and that therefore an unmanaged forest contributes nothing to reducing global CO_2?
... that wood retains its ability to bind CO_2 even after being used in homes and buildings?
... that processing wood requires smaller amounts of fossil fuels than processing other materials, such as steel and concrete, and thus releases far less CO_2?
... that making one cubic meter of aluminum releases 22 metric tons of CO_2, compared to 0.015 metric tons for sawn timber?
... that processing wood produces no waste, but rather reusable by-products?

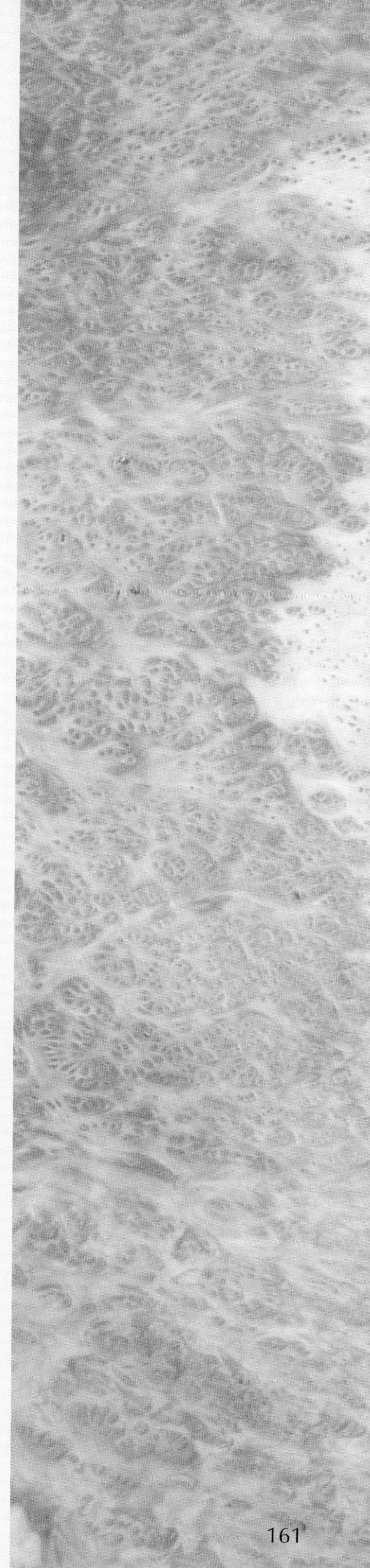

Appendix B
Figure Glossary

NOTE: A photo follows the description.

The following are examples of typical veneer figure types or classifications, along with descriptive words. The descriptive words are noted with an * and should not be confused with the veneer classifications. For example; when ordering crotch mahogany, the crotch defines the figure type, other descriptive words to help explain how the crotch look might be; "a broad roaster tail with intense flame and chatoyance." (See below for definitions) Each veneer sales person will have their own idea and interpretation of what these descriptive words visually mean, but they can help generate a closer visual description when ordering.

Below are typical figure names and descriptions that can be helpful when ordering material. *Courtesy of Certainly Wood Veneer.*

Angel Steps: (Quartered Etimoe) Refers to a type of curl often from a stump and/or butt sections of trees, producing a diagonal, staircase like curl.

Bee's Wing: (Satinwood) Smaller and more intense than mottled figure although structurally similar, bee's-wing figure is said to resemble that insect's appendage when magnified. (I haven't actually compared them.) East Indian satinwood, shown, is well known for having this figure, and it also occurs occasionally in narra, mahogany, and eucalyptus.

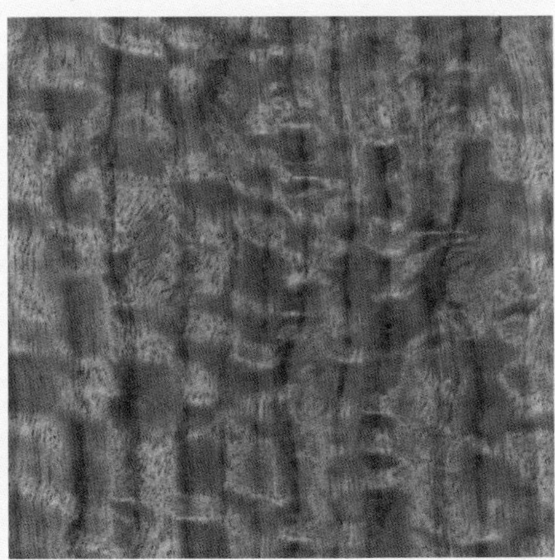

Bird's-Eye: (Maple) The name itself describes it best. Once considered a defect, the best bird's-eye flitches are now expensive and in demand. These veneers are most often rotary cut or half-round sliced (in an arc) to produce the most uniform distribution of nice round eyes. Bird's-eye is most common in maple (shown), but bird's-eye does occur in a few other species.

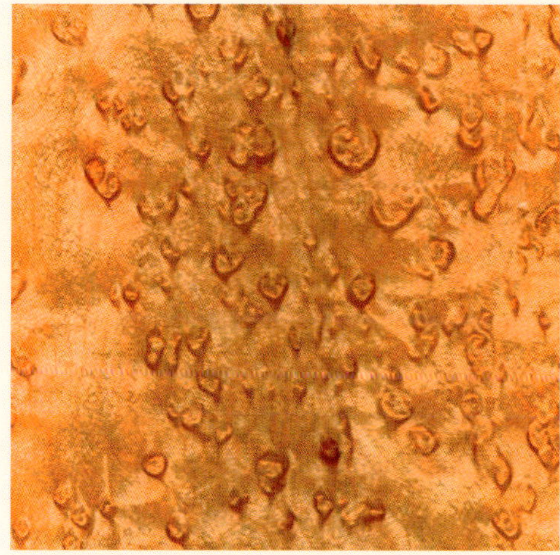

Blister: (Maple) A larger figure version of quilted. Billowing or bubble formation, often three dimensional looking.

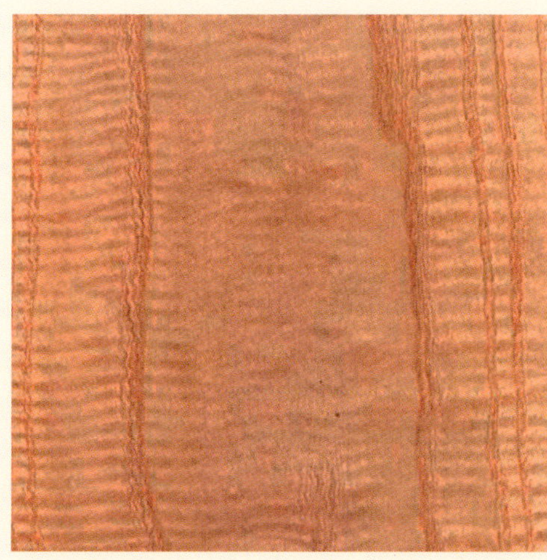

Burl: (Olive Ash) Growths on trees produce some of the most prized veneers. Usually available in smallish, often defective sheets, burls feature swirling grain around clusters of dormant buds, rings or eyes. Varieties include "cluster burl" or "cat's paw burl." Redwood, oak, ash, madrone, elm (shown), and walnut are common burl species; exotic burls include mappa, thuya, and amboyna.

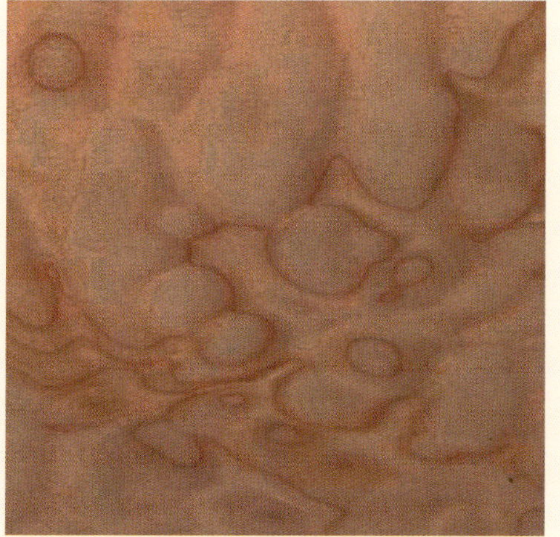

Broken Strip: (White Ash) Occurs when a figure, most often a curl appears to dive away from the face disappearing and reappearing as it come to the surface. This creates a broken or dashed figure strip.

Button: (Satinwood) When woods with large medullary rays are quartersawn, the harder, shinier rays are more fully exhibited and show up as "snowflakes" or buttons on a straight-grained background. Some veneer species, such as white oak, lacewood (shown), and American sycamore, are more attractive when sliced to reveal this button figure.

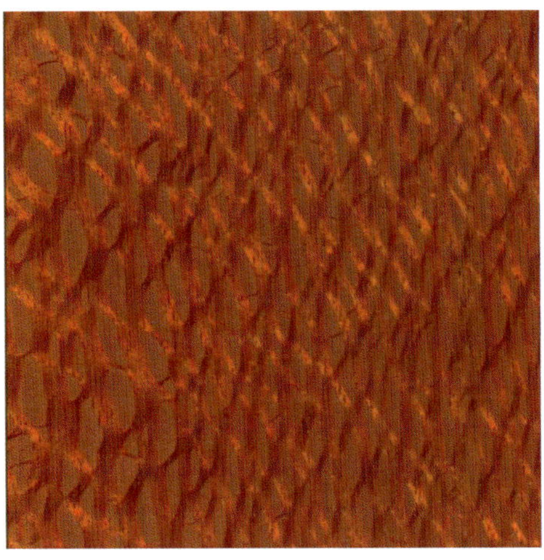

***Cat's Paw:** (Mappa Burl) The description for grouping of knot representing cat paw foot prints. Typically a description for burls but can also used to help justify / define odd and random knots and groupings.

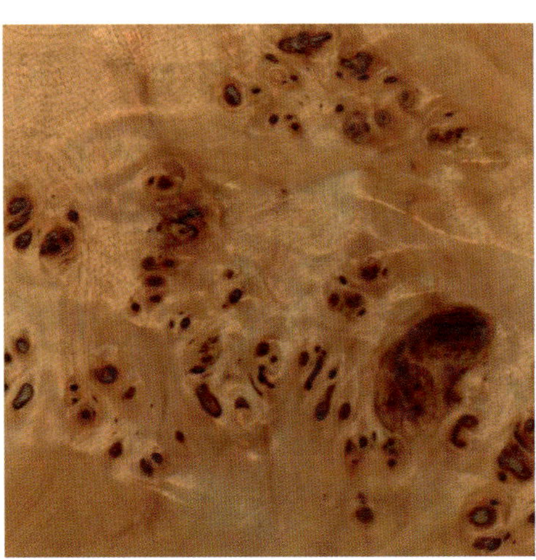

***Chatoyance:** (Paldao) This visual effect can give wood a three dimensional appearance, often making parts of the grain look lighter or darker when viewed from different angles. It is caused by how light reflects off the different density of woods. Coined from the French "oeil de shat", meaning "cat's eye."

***Cluster:** (Maple Burl) A term used to describe the tightness or density of a burl's figure.

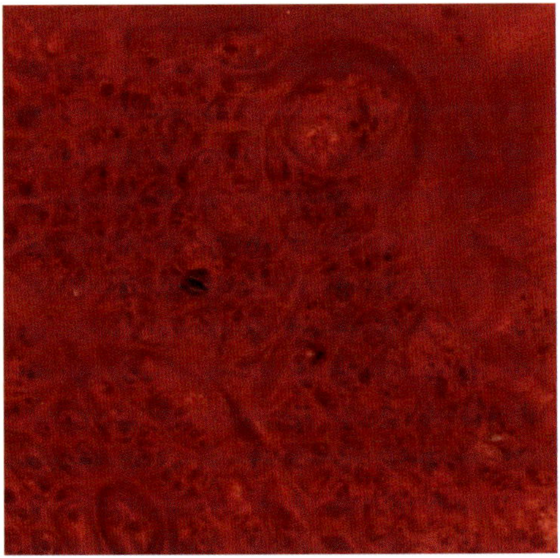

Crotch: (Mahogany) Cut from the juncture of a tree's main branches and trunk, crotch figures are often sub-categorized as flame, plume, rooster tail, feather or burning bush. All of these descriptive terms serve to convey the range of this figure's appearance. Seldom found in larger sizes, mahogany (shown) and walnut species dominate the field of crotch veneers.

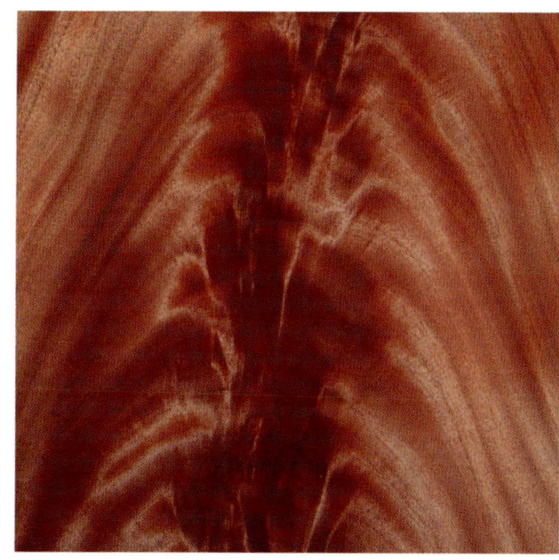

Curly: (Maple) Contortions in grain direction that reflect light differently create an appearance of undulating waves known as curly grain. Many species develop this figure, but most commonly maple, shown. Stump and butt sections of trees often produce a diagonal, staircaselike curl referred to as "angel steps," and a rolling curl figure that is called "cross-fire."

Fiddleback: (Makore) An estimable variation of curly figure, this figure's name is taken from its customary use for violin backs. Logs for fiddleback veneers are quartersawn to produce very straight grain with nearly perpendicular curls running uninterrupted from edge to edge. Maple, makore (shown), anigre, and English sycamore head a list of about 12 fiddleback-prone species.

***Flame**: (Redwood Burl) This term is often used to describe the level of chatoyance within a crotch, synonymous to fiery. It can also be used to describe the contrasting seam between the heartwood and sapwood. The seam transitions in a flame- like pattern. This effect (shown) is most often found in burl such as redwood and walnut.

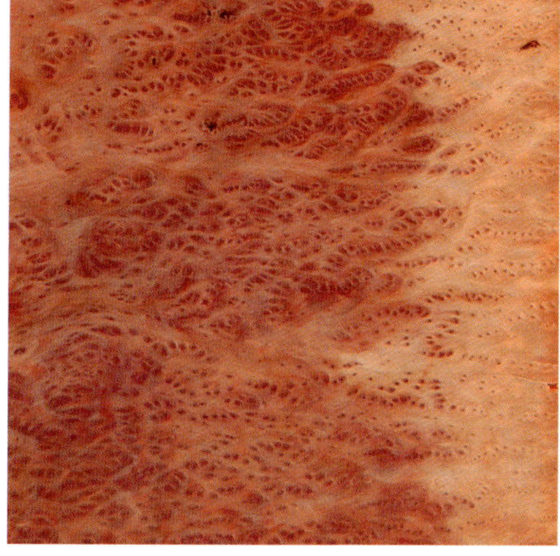

***Flat Cut or Plain Sliced:** (Ash) Type of cut (see page 16) which will typically yield cathedral grain pattern. Often in the center with more straight grain (rift cut) on the perimeter.

Knotty: (Chilean Laurel) A general term that expresses a large amount of small knots. It can refer to any size although typically conveys a relatively consistent spread.

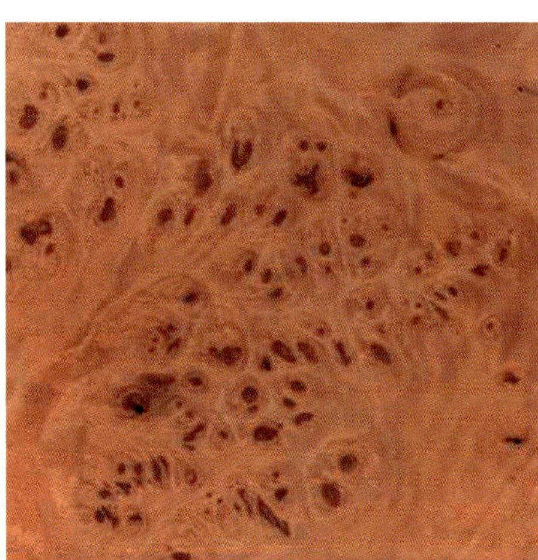

***Medullary Rays:** (White Oak; Quarter Sawn) Part of the tree's cellular structure that radiates from the center of the tree. They typically reveal themselves with a quarter sawn cut and are only prominent in some species. These harder, shinier rays are more fully exhibited and show up on a straight-grained background. Some veneer species, such as white oak (shown), lacewood, and American sycamore, are more attractive when sliced to reveal these rays.

Mottled: (Satinwood) Wavy grain combines with spiral, interlocked grain to produce a wrinkled, blotchy figure known as mottle. The mottled figure may be scattered randomly (broken mottle), or appear as a regular checkerboard pattern (block mottle). Members of the mahogany family, koa, sapele, bubinga, and African satinwood (shown), most commonly exhibit mottled figure.

Muscle: (Mappa Burl) Tight, swirly curl with high levels of chatoyance.

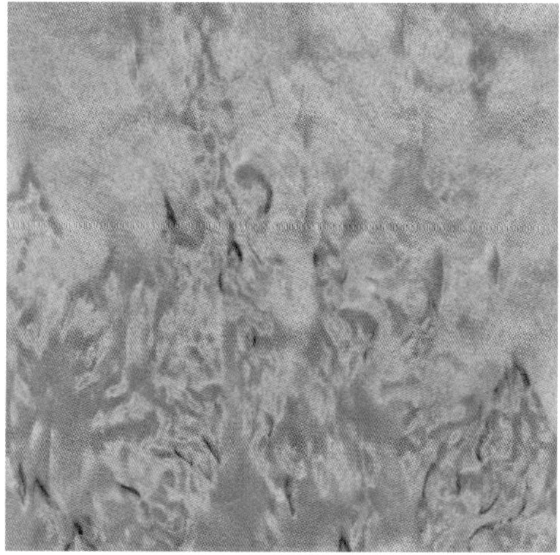

Peanut Shell: (Tamo Ash) When certain woods exhibit a quilted or blistered figure, they are rotary cut to promote a random, wild grain pattern as well. This peanut-shell grain creates a visual illusion similar to quilted figure: the veneer appears bumpy and pitted, when in fact it's flat. Tamo (Japanese ash shown), and bubinga are the two most popular examples of this figure.

Pommele: (Sapele) This figure resembles a puddle surface during a light rain: a dense pattern of small rings enveloping one another. Some say this has a "suede" or "furry" look. It's usually found in extremely large trees of African species like sapele (shown), bubinga, and makore. Some domestic species with a sparser, larger figure are referred to as "blistered."

Quilted: (Maple) Although greatly resembling a larger and exaggerated version of pommele or blister figure, quilted figure has bulges that are elongated and closely crowded. Quilted grain looks veritably three-dimensional when seen at its billowy best. It's most commonly found in mahogany, moabi, maple (shown), sapele, and myrtle, and occurs only rarely in other species.

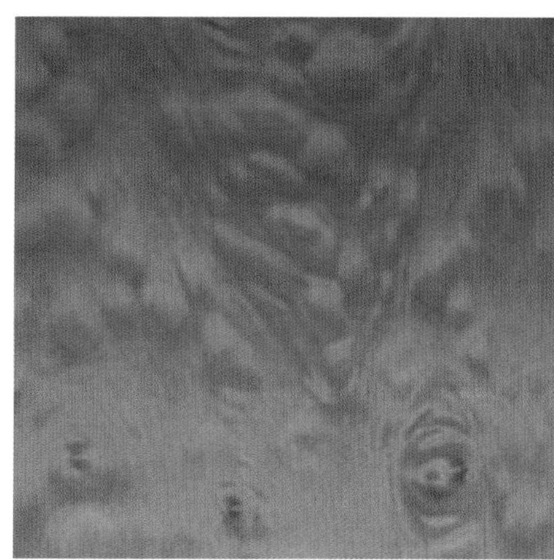

Ribbon Stripe: (Sapele) From a quarter sawn cut, it yields a predominate and consistent straight striping with a significant chatoyant effect.

Rifted: (Anigre) Type of cut that yields straight "combed" grain with no medullary rays.

Ropey: (Cherry) Large rolling curls often found in cherry.

Seagrass: (Mahogany) Large waving curls often found in mahogany.

Spalted: (Maple) Wood that has been discolored typically by fungi. After veneer slicing the mildew appears as pencil lines of black and grey in addition to often blotchy areas of color variation. Also referred to as Ambrosia.

***Straight Grain:** (Wenge) This term should not be used to only define a veneer; there are many types of cut that can produce a straight grain. Each may have other properties, such as quarter sawn that can reveal medullary rays or rift cut that will produce a very straight combed grain.

Swirl: (Walnut) This figure is a visually gentler version of regular crotch figure. As the name implies, the grain meanders and swirls around, often seeming to convolute and fold in upon itself. The densest portions of the swirl show up darker or shaded compared to the lighter surrounding wood. Swirl occurs in species including walnut (shown), mahogany, cherry, and maple.

Variegated: (Red Maple) A term to describe a multi color veneer. This can be a consistent zebra type striping or only a few contrasting lines (shown). Also know as spalted or ambrosia.

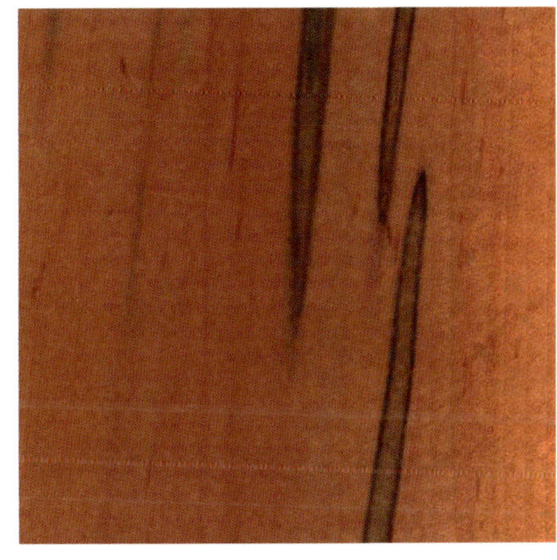

Wormy: (Chestnut) Wood that has been attacked by worms and/or beetles leaving tiny holes in the sheets of veneer

Appendix C
Glossary

Acrylic: Clear plastic panel used for making templates or translucent veneer panels.

Aniline Powder: Powdered dye stains that can be mixed with a variety of solvents, often used for color touch up repairs.

Balanced Panel: Panels that have similar material glued to each side to prevent warping.

Blendal® Pigment: A brand of aniline powder by Mohawk Finishing Supplies.

Board Feet (BF): A measurement of rough solid lumber. 1 BF = 12″ x 12″ x 1″

Breather Fabric: A mesh that is use to vent a panel within a vacuum bag.

Burl: An abnormal growth often found on a base of a tree or within the root system.

CA Glue: see Cyanoacrylate Glue

Caul: A flat panel or stiff board used in clamping.

CFM (Cubic Feet per Minute): A unit of measure for measuring the volume of air movement.

Chatoyance: The visual effect that can give wood a three dimensional appearance, often making parts of the grain to look lighter or darker when viewed from different angles. It is caused by light reflecting off the different densities within the wood.

Chipboard: An engineered wood panel used for a veneer core made from wood particles and glue. Also referred as flake board, particle board.

Clipped: Manufacturing term for cutting veneer edges, typically to cut off unwanted material.

Closed Pore: A term for a type of finish where the wood pores are filled. It is typically used for high gloss mirror finishes.

Cold Pressing: Refers to a type of gluing as opposed to a type of pressing with heat.

Conditioning: Processing veneer to soften the wood fibers.

Creep: Movement in wood veneer after it has been pressed and glued to a core.

Critical Alignment: The exact alignment of two pieces of veneer, often when a significant grain pattern needs to match up in a book match pattern.

Cubic Feet Per Minute: see CFM

Cull: To sort and remove material from a group.

Cyanoacrylate Glue: A fast acting glue or "instant glue" used for quick repairs or solidifying wood or stone dust in inlays.

De-Gassing: A liquid that expels gas either naturally or through forced methods, similar to a Champagne bottle "pop" when opening.

Double Bevel Cut: A method of seaming two pieces of veneer by cutting through both pieces of veneer at the same time using an angled cut.

EMT: electrical conduit (metal pipe) used for channeling electrical wire.

Famowood™: Brand of wood putty.

Fissures: Small cracks found in veneer.

Flake Board: see Chip Board.

Flattening: A process of flattening or conditioning veneer.

Flex Board: An engineered panel that is flexible.

Flush Trim Bit: A router bit with a bearing that aligns flush with the cutter. It trims overhanging material flush with its substrate.

Fret Saw: A handheld saw, typically with a fine blade and a deep throat.

Gap Filling: A material that fills a void, typically a rigid-curing glue.

Glue Line: The cured glue between two surfaces.

Grades: A rating system for wood or veneer.

Grain Drift: Natural transition of sequential grain pattern from leaf to leaf.

Honeycomb Panel: A panel with a honeycomb interior, which makes the panel lightweight and strong.

Join: A method used to straighten an edge of lumber or veneer.

Kerf: A void created from a saw blade when cutting wood.

Lay Up: Term for combining glue and wood for pressing.

Leaf Shift: Veneer leaves that shift as they are cut off the log, which can drastically affect the grain alignment.

Lignum: Natural resin within wood that holds the fibers together.

Marquetry: The technique of applying wood veneer to a substructure to form patterns or pictures.

Masonite: An engineered board made from wood fiber that is steamed and pressed together with no glue. The panels are typically thin; the surface is harder than particle board and is good for bending.

MDF: see Medium Density Fiberboard.

Medium Density Fiberboard: Engineered panel made from fine sawdust and glue.

Mineral Stains: Dark stains in wood caused by natural minerals. They can be random small stripes or larger discolored areas.

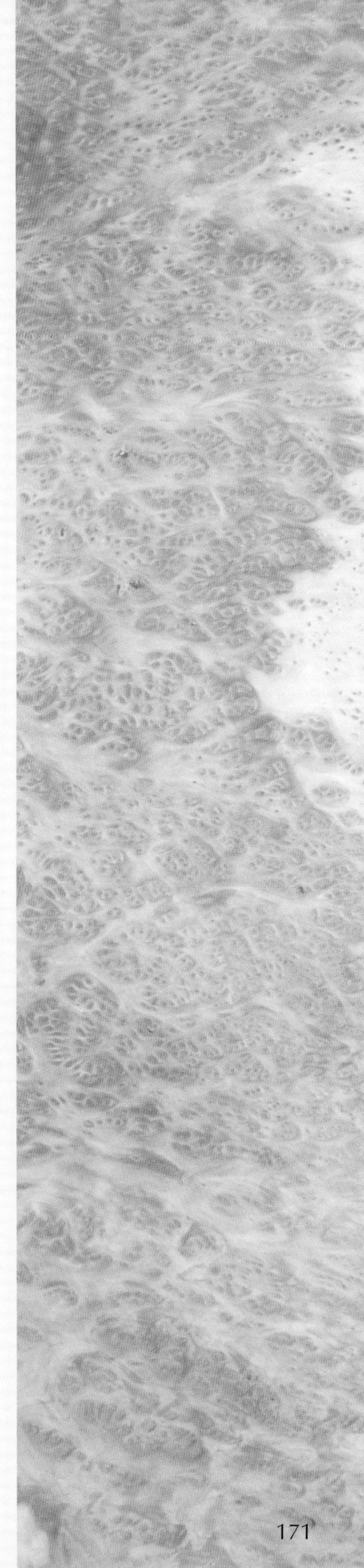

Molding Grade: Finest grade of MDF with higher tolerances. Cut edges will be cleaner with minimal fuzz and chipping.

Mylar: A thin plastic film, typically clear.

Non-Perf Tape: Veneer tape that is solid; opposed to perforated tape, with holes.

Open Time: The amount of time it takes between applying or catalyzing glue and the time it becomes ineffective or unable to create a bond.

Orbital Sander: A sander with a circular sanding pad. The circular motion spins in two ways, a circle and an ellipse, which ensures that the sanding grit will not travel in the same path. This type of sander is also known as a dual action sander or D.A. sander.

Overlap Cutting: When two layers of veneer are overlapped and cut at once, typically cut in place to perfectly align a seam, often used in hot hide hammer gluing.

Packs: A group or bundle of veneer.

Pallet: A flat wooden structure used for shipping material.

Particle board: see Chip Board.

Perf Tape: Veneer tape with holes punched through.

Phenolic: Paper impregnated with a synthetic (phenolic) resin and pressed under high pressure to create a strong and stable material.

Plane: A tool or process to flatten a surface or edge.

Platen: Flat panel use to channel air from within a vacuum bag.

Primary colors: Red, Blue, Yellow, from which all other colors can be created.

Poly Vinyl Acetate: type of water-based glue, typically known as white or yellow glue.

PVA: see Poly Vinyl Acetate

Radial Match: a pattern match where the seams all converge to one center point.

Sanding Swirls: Tiny scrapes left behind from sanding.

Sapwood: The outer portion of a tree, typically lighter in color.

Scarf Joint: A steep angled glue seam.

Scraper: A thin piece of metal with a burr on its edge used for smoothing wood in lieu of sanding.

Scroll Saw: A power saw with a fine blade, typically with a deep throat and used for intricate cutting and tight radii.

Secondary Colors: Green, Orange, Purple, made from mixing two primary colors.

Shadowing: A contrasting area (lighter or darker) or discoloration of wood created by bleaching or darkening due to light exposure or oxidation.

Shellac: A resin secreted from a female lac bug. Dried resin flakes are dissolved in denatured alcohol to make a liquid, used as a sealer or light duty finish.

Sketch Face: A field or panel made from multiple pieces of veneer.

Slicing Score Lines: Linear lines in veneer created from the cutting knife. They often appear as indentations on one side of the veneer and bumps on the opposite side.

Stack Cutting: A stack of veneer pressed together to essentially form a single block of wood which is cut all at once.

Sticker: Separating stacks of panels or lumber with thin sticks to create voids for ventilation. A method used to evenly dry panels or lumber.

Stir™: A brand of machinery, know for pneumatic sanders.

Straight Line: Directional sanding, back and forth.

Stringers: Structural stair supports.

Sunburst: A pattern of veneer that radiates from a center point.

Super Glue: see Cyanoacrylate Glue.

Tape Shadows: A contrasting area (lighter or darker) or discoloration of wood created by bleaching or darkening due to light exposure or oxidation.

TEC: See Thermal Expansion Coefficient

Telegraph: A surface deflection or bump that is transferred from particles or seam movement from under a material.

Thermal Expansion Coefficient: the rate of movement due to a change in its temperature.

Value: The lightness or darkness of a color, i.e. a darker value of red is brown.

Veneer: A thin slice of wood, typically 1/42 of an inch thick.

Venturi: A device also referred to an aspirator that creates a vacuum, or a tube that gradually narrows, as air moves through it, which creates a vacuum by means of the venturi effect.

Wiggle Board: Thin plywood where the grain runs in the same direction allowing the panel to bend with the grain.

Witness Line: Faint seam lines or haze created from sanding through different layers of finish with different sheens.

Wood Blank: A large section of lumber, typically a half or quarter of a tree.

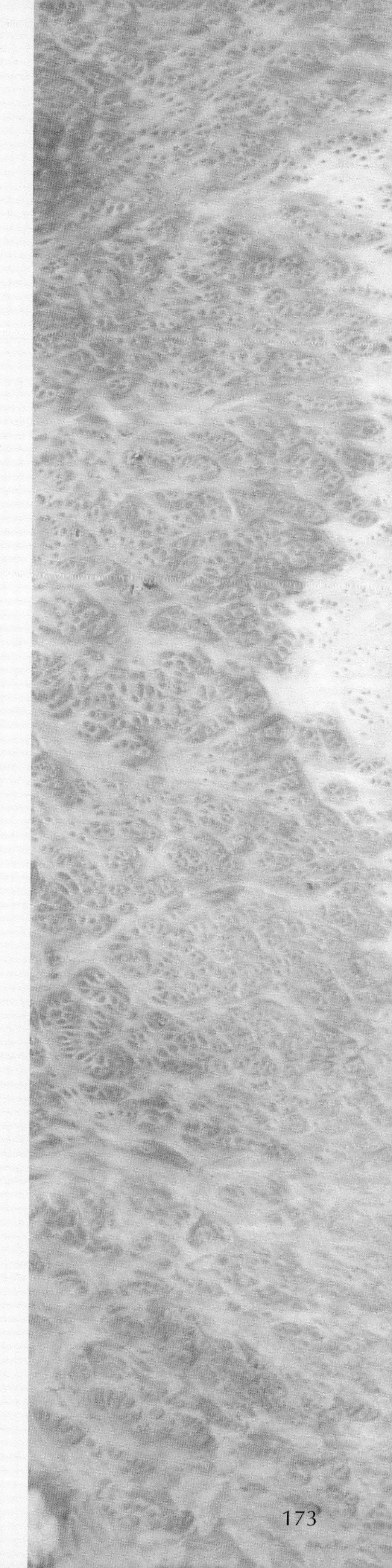

Appendix D
Resources

Associations

American Architectural Manufacturers Association – AAMA
1827 Walden Office Square, Suite 550
Schaumburg, Illinois 60173-4268
(847) 303-5664; (847) 303-5774 fax
http://www.aamanet.org/

American Forest & Paper Association
1111 Nineteenth Street, NW
Suite 800
Washington, DC 20036
(800) 878-8878; (202) 463-2700
info@afandpa.org
http://www.afandpa.org/

American Society of Furniture Designers
Christine Evans, Executive Director
Headquarters:
144 Woodland Drive
New London, NC 28127
(910) 576-1273
http://www.asfd.com

American Wood Council
803 Sycolin Road, Suite 201
Leesburg, VA 20175
(202) 463 2766
publications@awc.org

Architectural Woodwork Institute
46179 Westlake Drive, Suite 120,
Potomac Falls, VA 20165
(571)323-3636; (571)323-3630 fax
http://www.awinet.org

Association of Woodworking & Furnishings Suppliers - AWSF
500 Citadel Drive, Suite 200
Commerce, CA 90040
(323)838-9440
http://www.awfs.org

Cabinet Makers Association - CMA
PO Box 14276
Milwaukee, WI 53214
(414) 377-1350
http://www.cabinetmakers.org

Composite Panel Association
19465 Deerfield Avenue, Suite 306
Leesburg, VA 20176
(703) 724-1128
http://www.pbmdf.com

The Council of Forest Industries
1501-700 West Pender Street
Pender Place I Business Building
Vancouver, BC
Canada, V6C 1G8
(604) 684-0211
http://www.cofi.org

Convention on International Trade of Endangered Species - CITES
11 Chemin des Anémones
CH-1219 Châtelaine, Geneva
Switzerland
41-(0)22-917-81-39/40
http://www.cites.org/

Forest Products Society
2801 Marshall Ct.
Madison, WI 53705-2295 USA
(608) 231-1361
(608) 231-2152 (fax)
http://www.forestprod.org

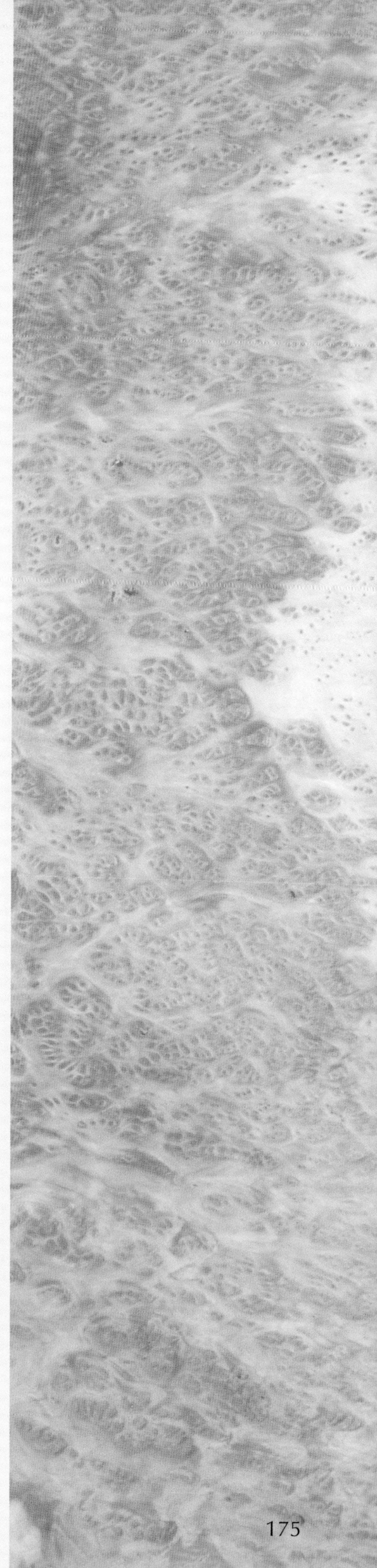

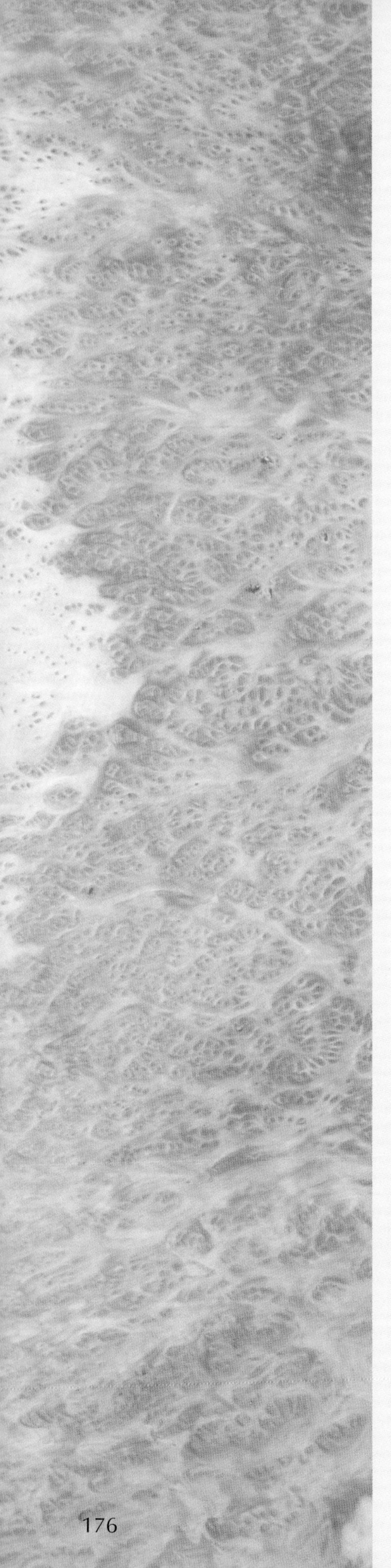

Forest Resources Association Inc. (FRA)
600 Jefferson Plaza, Suite 350
Rockville, MD 20852
(301) 838-9385
http://www.forestresources.org

The International Woodworking Fair
3520 Piedmont Rd. NE, Suite 350
Atlanta, Georgia 30305
(404)693-8333
(404)693-8350 fax
iwf@iwfatlanta.com
http://www.iwfatlanta.com

WoodIndustryEd.org
c/o AWFS
500 Citadel Drive, Suite 200
Commerce, CA 90040
(323) 838-9440 or (800) 946-2937
http://www.woodindustryed.org

Wood Machinery Manufacturers of America - WMMA®
500 Citadel Drive, Suite 200
Commerce, CA 90040
(323) 215-0330 or (847) 303-5664
(323) 215-0331 fax
info@wmma.org

WOODWEB, Inc.
335 Bedell Road
Montrose, PA 18801
(570) 278-5315
http://www.woodweb.com/

Woodwork Institute
P.O. Box 980247
West Sacramento, CA 95798
(916) 372-9943
http://www.woodworkinstitute.com

Woodworking Machinery Industry Association
3313 Paper Mill Road Suite 202
Phoenix, MD 21131
(410) 628-1970; (410) 628-1972
http://wmia.org